The Persian Empire from Cyrus II to Artaxerxes I

Second Edition

LACTOR Sourcebooks in Ancient History

For more than half a century, *LACTOR Sourcebooks in Ancient History* have been providing for the needs of students at schools and universities who are studying ancient history in English translation. Each volume focuses on a particular period or topic and offers a generous and judicious selection of primary texts in new translations. The texts selected include not only extracts from important literary sources but also numerous inscriptions, coin legends and extracts from legal and other texts, which are not otherwise easy for students to access. Many volumes include annotation as well as a glossary, maps and other relevant illustrations, and sometimes a short Introduction. The volumes are written and reviewed by experienced teachers of ancient history at both schools and universities. The series is now being published in print and digital form by Cambridge University Press, with plans for both new editions and completely new volumes.

Osborne	*The Athenian Empire*
Osborne	*The Old Oligarch*
Cooley	*Cicero's Consulship Campaign*
Grocock	*Inscriptions of Roman Britain*
Osborne	*Athenian Democracy*
Santangelo	*Late Republican Rome, 88-31 BC*
Warmington/Miller	*Inscriptions of the Roman Empire, AD 14-117*
Treggiari	*Cicero's Cilician Letters*
Rathbone/Rathbone	*Literary Sources for Roman Britain*
Sabben-Clare/Warman	*The Culture of Athens*
Stockton	*From the Gracchi to Sulla*
Edmondson	*Dio: the Julio-Claudians*
Brosius	*The Persian Empire from Cyrus II to Artaxerxes I*
Cooley/Wilson	*The Age of Augustus*
Levick	*The High Tide of Empire*
Cooley	*Tiberius to Nero*
Cooley	*The Flavians*
Cooley	*Sparta*

The Persian Empire from Cyrus II to Artaxerxes I

Second Edition

Translated and edited with notes by
MARIA BROSIUS
University of Newcastle upon Tyne

CAMBRIDGE
UNIVERSITY PRESS

Shaftesbury Road, Cambridge CB2 8EA, United Kingdom

One Liberty Plaza, 20th Floor, New York, NY 10006, USA

477 Williamstown Road, Port Melbourne, VIC 3207, Australia

314–321, 3rd Floor, Plot 3, Splendor Forum, Jasola District Centre, New Delhi – 110025, India

103 Penang Road, #05–06/07, Visioncrest Commercial, Singapore 238467

Cambridge University Press is part of Cambridge University Press & Assessment, a department of the University of Cambridge.

We share the University's mission to contribute to society through the pursuit of education, learning and research at the highest international levels of excellence.

www.cambridge.org
Information on this title: www.cambridge.org/9781009382946
DOI: 10.1017/9781009382977

First published 2023

A catalogue record for this publication is available from the British Library.

A Cataloging-in-Publication data record for this book is available from the Library of Congress.

ISBN 978-1-009-38294-6 Paperback

Cambridge University Press & Assessment has no responsibility for the persistence or accuracy of URLs for external or third-party internet websites referred to in this publication and does not guarantee that any content on such websites is, or will remain, accurate or appropriate.

ACKNOWLEDGEMENTS

I wish to thank several scholars who have read all or parts of the manuscript and who have assisted me with the translation of sources or improved readings of the texts. My particular thanks go to Heather Baker for the translations of Babylonian economic texts included in this volume, Elizabeth Tucker for her valuable notes and comments on the Old Persian texts, and John Baines for his helpful comments on the hieroglyphic documents. I am greatly indebted to John Roberts for his thorough reading of earlier drafts, and to Marion Cox, who drew the illustrations. I am grateful to the Director of the National Museum of Iran, Tehran, Mr. Mohammad Reza Kargar, for his permission to reproduce the photograph of the statue of Darius I, and to Ian Mathieson and the Egypt Exploration Society, who kindly gave permission to reproduce a photograph of the funerary stele from Saqqara. Finally, I thank Pauline Hire and Cambridge University Press for permission to reproduce the map of the Persian empire from *CAH* IV (1988).

M.B.

Warm thanks are due to Robin Osborne for all he did to prepare the final draft for the press.

The publication of LACTOR 16 marks the start of a period of expansion, prompted by the introduction of the new AS and A levels in September of this year.

May 2000

John Roberts
General Editor

TABLE OF CONTENTS
(Numbers in bold print refer to passages) *Page*

PART I. The Rise of Persia

PART II. The Persian Empire under the first three Achaemenid Kings

**PART III. The Organisation and Administration of the Persian Empire;
Religion in the Empire**

Map and List of Illustrations

Map

Illustrations

Notes and Abbreviations

All dates are B.C. unless otherwise stated.

Translations of Old Persian texts are adapted from Kent unless otherwise stated. The text of the Inscription of Bisitun is based on the Old Persian version translated by Rüdiger Schmitt, and also has taken into account the Babylonian version translated by Elizabeth von Voigtlander, and the Elamite version translated by François Vallat. Greek translations are adapted from the Loeb editions. To facilitate the reading of the Babylonian texts, diacritics have been omitted. The letter š is to read as [sh].

Square brackets in quoted passages indicate a restored reading of the text. Additions to the text inserted to facilitate its reading are marked by round brackets. Words or comments made by the editor as an aid to improve understanding of the text are printed in italics in round brackets.

Abbreviations of Books and Journals

AchHist   Achaemenid History (Leiden): vol viii: *Continuity and Change*, ed. H. Sancisi-Weerdenburg, A. Kuhrt, and M.C. Root (1994); vol. 11: *Studies in Persian History. Essays in Memory of David M. Lewis*, ed. M. Brosius and A. Kuhrt (1998).

AcIr   *Acta Iranica* (Leiden)

AION   *Annali dell'Istituto Orientale di Napoli* (Naples)

AMI   *Archäologische Mitteilungen aus Iran* (Berlin)

ANET   *Ancient Near Eastern Texts Relating to the Old Testament* ed. J.B. Pritchard, 2nd edition (Princeton, 1955)

ASAE   *Annales de Service des antiquités d'Egypte* (Paris)

BE   *The Babylonian Expedition of the University of Pennsylvania, Series A: Cuneiform Texts*, vol. IX (1898): A.V. Hilprecht and A.T. Clay, *Business Documents of Murashû Sons of Nippur dated to the Reign of Artaxerxes I* (Philadelphia)

Cah D.A.F.I.   *Cahiers de la délégation archéologique française en Iran* (Paris)

FGrH   *Die Fragmente der griechischen Historiker*, ed. F. Jacoby (Berlin and Leiden 1923-58)

Fornara   *Archaic times to the end of the Peloponnesian War*, ed. C.W. Fornara, 2nd edition (Cambridge, 1983).

IrAnt   *Iranica Antiqua* (Leiden)

JHS   *Journal of Hellenic Studies* (London)

JNES   *Journal of Near Eastern Studies* (Chicago)

JSOT   *Journal for the Study of the Old Testament* (Sheffield)

MDP   Mémoires de la Délégation en Perse

ML   *A Selection of Greek Historical Inscriptions to the end of the fifth century B.C.*, ed. R. Meiggs and D.M. Lewis, revised edition (Oxford, 1988).

RA   *Revue d'assyriologie* (Paris)

StIr   *Studia Iranica* (Paris)

VS	*Vorderasiatische Schriftdenkmäler der Königlichen Museen zu Berlin* (Leipzig)
ZA	*Zeitschrift für Assyriologie* (Berlin)
ZDMG	*Zeitschrift der deutschen morgenländischen Gesellschaft* (Wiesbaden)

Abbreviations of Persian Sources

A^{1}I	Inscription of Artaxerxes I on a silver dish
A^{1}Orsk	Inscription of Artaxerxes I from Orsk
A^{1}Pa	Inscription of Artaxerxes I from Persepolis
AmH	Inscription of Ariaramnes from Hamadan
AsH	Inscription of Arsames from Hamadan
CMa	Inscription of Cyrus II from Murghab (a)
DB	Darius inscription of Bisitun
DE	Darius inscription from Mount Elvand
DNa	Darius inscription from Naqš-e Rustam (a)
DNb	Darius inscription from Naqš-e Rustam (b)
DNc	Darius inscription from Naqš-e Rustam (c)
DNd	Darius inscription from Naqš-e Rustam (d)
DPd	Darius inscription from Persepolis (d)
DPe	Darius inscription from Persepolis (e)
DPh	Darius inscription from Persepolis (h)
DSab	Darius inscription from Susa (ab)
DSe	Darius inscription from Susa (e)
DSf	Darius inscription from Susa (f)
DZc	Darius inscription from the Red Sea Canal (c)
Fort.	Fortification Texts (collated by G.G. Cameron)
PF	Persepolis Fortification Texts, 1969
PFa	Persepolis Fortification Texts, 1978
PF-NN	Persepolis Fortification Texts, Manuscript Hallock
PFS	Persepolis Fortification Seals
PT	Persepolis Treasury Texts
PTS	Persepolis Treasury Seals
SDa	Seal of Darius
SXe	Seal inscription of Xerxes (e)
SXf	Seal inscription of Xerxes (f)
XE	Xerxes inscription from Mount Elvand
XPa	Xerxes inscription from Persepolis (a)
XPf	Xerxes inscription from Persepolis (f)
XPh	Xerxes inscription from Persepolis (h)
XV	Xerxes inscription from Lake Van

Other Abbreviations and Symbols

Bab.	Babylonian
BM	British Museum

BN	Bibliothèque Nationale
ed.	edited by
Elam.	Elamite
Gr.	Greek
Hier.	Hieroglyphics
l., ll.	line, lines
lit.	literally
OP	Old Persian
pl.	plural
⌈ ⌉	reading partially restored
[ ]	lacuna
( )	amendment to or omission from the text
!	unusual or inaccurate sign form or use of script
?	uncertain reading
*	reconstructed form

Alphabetical List of Near Eastern Texts

Text Reference	Edition or Title	Passage no.
Old Persian Inscriptions		
A¹I	Kent 1953	77
A¹Orsk	Mayrhofer 1978	78
A¹ Pa	Kent 1953	76
A¹Pa:§2	Kent 1953	102
AmH	Kent 1953	2
AsH	Kent 1953	3
CMa	Kent 1953	4
DB	Schmitt 1991	44
DB I: §1		99
DB I: §10		30
DB.I: §11		27
DB I: §11-15		35
DB III: §38		123
DB III: §45		124
DE	Kent 1953	47
DNa	Kent 1953	48
DNa:§2		100
DNa: §3		136
DNb	Lecoq 1997	103
DNc	Kent 1953	112
DNd	Kent 1953	113
DPd	Kent 1953	104
DPe	Kent 1953	133
DPh	Kent 1953	134
DSab	Kent 1953	49
DSe	Kent 1953	46
DSf	Grillot-Susini 1990	45
DZc	Kent 1953	52
SDa	Schmitt 1981	43
SXe	Schmitt 1981	62
SXf	Schmitt 1981	61
XE	Kent 1953	65
XPa	Kent 1953	63
XPa: §2		101
XPf: §4	Kent 1953	107
XPh	Kent 1953	191
XPh: §3		135
XV	Kent 1953	64
Babylonian texts		
BE IX 109		91
BM 74554	Stolper 1989	130
Cyrus Cylinder	Berger 1975	12

Alphabetical List of Greek and Roman Authors

Author	Title of work	Reference	Passage no.
Aeschylus	*Persians*	774-777	31
Aristotle	*Politics*	1311b37-40	74
Arrian	*Anabasis*	3.27.4	118
Ctesias	*Persica*	FGrH 688 F 1	10
		FGrH 688 F 9	34, 120
		FGrH 688 F 13	29, 40, 73
		FGrH 688 F 14	83
		FGrH 688 F 15	92
Diodorus Siculus		11.69.1-2	75
		11.69.2-6	81
		11.71-77	88
		12.4.5	90
		12.64.1	93
Herodotus		1.53	14
		1.86.1	15
		1.107.1-2	6
		1.125.3	5
		1.127	13
		1.131-132	199
		1.136	105
		1.153.3-154	16
		1.183.2-3	200
		2.158.1-2	53
		3.2.2	176
		3.12.4	84
		3.17	25
		3.25.4-26.3	26
		3.27.-3.30.1	23
		3.30	32
		3.61	36
		3.64.3-4	28
		3.67.2-3	37
		3.70	38
		3.78.4-5	39
		3.84.1	121
		3.88.2-3	177
		3.97.1	139
		3.140.1	116
		3.160	85
		4.166.1	125
		5.52.1-53	181
		6.43.1	179
		6.43.4-44.1	57
		6.48.1-49.1	58

Glossary

araššara	(Elam.), 'female chief (of workers)'
bāji	(OP), 'tribute' (including 'gifts')
barrišdama lakkukra	(Elam.), 'élite guide'
bazi uttibe	(Elam.), 'tax-handlers'
bullae	lumps of clay attached to a document and impressed with seals
cuneiform	form of writing in which the symbols are formed by wedge-shaped impressions
dahyāva	(OP), 'land', 'people'
daiva	(OP), 'demon'
Daric	Persian coin
dattibarra	(Elam.), 'law officer'
Demotic	popular Egyptian form of writing
dukšiš	(Elam.), 'princess'
dumme	(Elam.), 'copy'?
gorytus	(Gr.), 'quiver'
halmi	(Elam.), a sealed document used as authorisation for travellers in the Persian empire
halnut haššira	(Elam.), 'auditor'
haturmakša	(Elam.), 'fire-fanner'. A title for a Persian priest fulfilling a certain function in religious ceremonies
ka	(Hier.), in Egyptian religion the vitality of a man, which leaves the body at the point of death and is reunited with it in the after-world
karabattiš	(Elam.), 'caravan leader'
kurdabattiš	(Elam.), 'chief of workers'
lan	(Elam.), religious ceremony
mahišta	(OP), 'the greatest'
magus	*makuš* (Elam.), Persian priest celebrating the religious cults of western Iran
matištukkašp	(Elam.*)*, 'chiefs'
mušin zikkira	(Elam.), 'accountant'
ostraka	(Gr.) potsherds used in voting
parasang	Persian measure of distance (5-6 km)
partetaš	(Elam.), 'estates', 'garden', 'park'
pentekontor	(Gr.), ship with fifty oars
petasos	(Gr.) special type of felt hat worn by a group of Ionians
pihātu	(Bab.), 'governor'
pirradaziš	(Elam.), 'fast messenger'
pr-šn	(Hier.), variety of pine?
proskynesis	(Gr.), 'obeisance'. The Persians performed *proskynesis* before the king, either bowing their head and holding a hand in front of their mouth as a gesture of respect, or prostrating themselves.
rnp-priest	(Hier.), lit. 'youthful priest'
saris	*ša rēš šarri* (Akk.), 'master', 'governor'
šatin	(Elam.), 'priest'

satrap, satrapy	*xšaçapāvan* (OP), lit. 'protector of the realm'. The Persian empire was administered in satrapies or provinces, which were headed by a satrap, Persian governor.
stele	(Gr.), slab of stone on which an inscription or sculpture was carved
sunki pakri	(Elam.), 'daughter of the king'. This is the standard term of reference for a royal daughter, following the convention of earlier Near Eastern courts.

Notes on Near Eastern Sources (see also Note A pp.1f.)

The Persian Royal Inscriptions
The inscriptions written by the Achaemenid kings of Persia in Elamite, Babylonian and Old Persian cuneiform. Most of the royal inscriptions are dated to the reigns of Darius I and his successor Xerxes, though a few later inscriptions, dating from Artaxerxes I to Artaxerxes III, are also preserved. For explanations of the royal inscriptions see under the individual entries.

The Persepolis Fortification texts
During excavations in Persepolis in 1933/4, undertaken by members of the Oriental Institute of Chicago, over 30,000 clay tablets and fragments were found. They were part of an economic archive of Persepolis, concerned with the transfer and issuing of foodstuffs and livestock to individuals and groups of workers. The texts were written in Elamite cuneiform, a language and script which had been used in the administration of the kings of Elam. The texts are dated to the reign of Darius I, covering the period from 509 to 494. In 1969 R.T. Hallock published 2,087 texts (PF), and a further 33 in 1978 (PFa). Another 2,587 texts were transliterated by Hallock but remain unpublished (PF-NN, Manuscript Hallock).

The Persepolis Treasury texts
The tablets found by Ernst Schmidt during the excavation campaign of 1936/7 in a complex called the 'Treasury' were subsequently called the Treasury texts. This collection consists of 750 tablets and fragments, of which fewer than 100 are published as *Persepolis Treasury Tablets*. They are economic texts mainly concerned with the payment of workers. Like the Fortification texts, they are written in Elamite; they date between 492 and 458.

Other Near Eastern Sources
Explanations of other Near Eastern sources are given under the individual entries.

Notes on Greek and Roman Authors

Aeschylus (?525–456)
Tragic poet. In the *Persians*, performed in 472, he presented a hellenised version of the Persian court, emphasising the *hybris* of Xerxes and the decadence of Persia.

Aristotle (384–322)
Philosopher from Stageira in Chalcidice, wrote his *Politics* on the basis of a collection of 158 forms of government and state, among them the famous *Constitution of Athens*. The text of the *Politics* is a set of lecture notes.

Arrian
From Nicomedia in Bithynia, the historian served under the Roman emperor Hadrian. His historical works include a history of Parthia, *Parthika*, which was written in 17 books, but is now lost, the *Indike*, an account of Nearchus' voyage from South India to the Tigris, and, most notably, the *Anabasis*, a history of the campaigns of Alexander in Persia.

Berossus
He lived around the beginning of the third century BC in Babylon, where he was a priest of the city god Bel-Marduk. His history of Babylon, dedicated to the Seleucid king Antiochus I, was written in three books, covering events from the earliest period to the death of Alexander.

Ctesias
For seventeen years, from 405 onwards, Ctesias, a Greek doctor from Cnidus, lived at the court of Artaxerxes II. His history of Persia (*Persika*), written in 23 books, was widely used by ancient authors like Plato, Ephorus and Nicolaus of Damascus, though not without criticism because of his questionable treatment of historical facts. Despite its weaknesses, Ctesias' history has been proved to be correct on various aspects of Persian politics. His work survives only in the epitome of Photius of Byzantium.

Diodorus Siculus
A historian who lived in the first century BC at Agyrium in Sicily. He was certainly active between 60 and 36. His history is preserved in 40 books, written in annalistic form from the earliest times to Caesar's Gallic War. As he wrote for the Greco-Roman world, he combined the history of Greece and Rome with that of other countries. He draws from a number of sources, amongst them Hecataeus, Ctesias and Ephorus. He often lacks critical judgement in his presentation of events, summarises his source, and therefore omits details, and misdates events outside his chronological lists. However, he often provides information which we otherwise would not possess. For example, while Thucydides makes no mention of the Peace of Callias of 450/49, and Herodotus refers to it only indirectly, Diodorus is our main source for this important treaty between Athens and Persia.

Herodotus (Hdt.)
Herodotus lived from *c.* 484 until some years after the outbreak of the Peloponnesian War. Born in Halicarnassus in Caria, he experienced at first hand the life of Greeks

under Persian rule. His *Histories* are the primary source for the history of the Greek and Persian Wars of 490 and 480/479.

Justin
His epitome of the *Historiae Philippicae* of Pompeius Trogus was written in the 2nd or 3rd century AD. The text consists mostly of excerpts; his own added comments are anecdotal rather than factual. Over 200 manuscripts of his epitome are preserved from the Middle Ages, reflecting the fact that it was widely used as a school book.

Nicolaus of Damascus (born *c*.64)
Nicolaus was a court historian in the service of Herod the Great. His great work was a world history written in 144 books, the *Historiai*. The first seven books discussed the history of the Assyrians, Medes, Lydians and the Persians. The remaining volumes are only fragmentarily preserved, but recorded historical events to at least 7 BC.

Plato (428/7–349/8)
A follower of Socrates until his death in 399, Plato founded his own school of philosophy between 388 and 385. His work comprises several letters and 27 dialogues, most notably the *Republic* and the *Laws*.

Plutarch (before AD 50 – after AD 120)
Philosopher and biographer from Chaeronea, Boeotia. He is best known for his *Parallel Lives*, which are descriptions of the man's character rather than historical accounts. His work therefore often lacks critical analysis and an awareness of the political and historical context.

Strabo (64/3 BC – after AD 23)
A historian and geographer, Strabo originally came from Amaseia in Pontus. He was educated in Rome, then travelled to Egypt and back to Amaseia in c.7 BC where he remained until his death. His major work, the *Geographia*, is collected in seventeen books, with Books 12 to 15 focusing on Asia Minor and Persia, Books 16 and 17 on Mesopotamia and Egypt.

Thucydides (early 450's – *c*.400)
The family of the author of the *Peloponnesian War* came from Thrace, though they also were related to members of the Athenian aristocracy. The first book of the *Peloponnesian War* includes a historical outline of the *pentekontaetia*, the 50-year-period between 479 and 431, which includes references to events in Persia during the reigns of Xerxes and Artaxerxes I.

Xenophon (born between 430 – 425, d.355)
In 401 Xenophon and an army of 10,000 Greeks joined Cyrus the Younger in his revolt against his brother and king, Artaxerxes II. After their defeat at Cunaxa, the Greek army returned home, marching through Persian territory under Xenophon's leadership, an event he recorded in his *Anabasis*. His historical work, the *Hellenica*, begins with the events of 411/410, continuing where Thucydides' account of the *Peloponnesian War* breaks off. Neither a biography nor a history, his *Cyropaedia*, the 'Education of Cyrus', is a treatise on the upbringing and the reign of the Persian king Cyrus II, revealing considerable insight into Persian customs and life at the royal court.

Babylonian and Old Persian Calendars

Babylonian	Old Persian	
1. Nisannu	Adukani	(March/April)
2. Ayyaru	Thuravahara	(April/May)
3. Simannu	Thaigraciš	(May/June)
4. Du'zu	Garmapada	(June/July)
5. Abu	Turnabaziš	(July/August)
6. Ululu	Karbašiyaš	(August/September)
7. Tašritu	Bagayadiš	(September/October)
8. Arahšamnu	Varkazana	(October/November)
9. Kislimu	Açiyadiya	(November/December)
10. Tebetu	Anamaka	(December/January)
11. Šabatu	Samiyamaš	(January/February)
12. Addaru	Viyaxna	(February/March)

Weights and Measures

1 talent = 60 minas = 30 kg
1 mina = 60 shekels = 500g (of silver)
1 shekel = 1/60 mina
1 karsha = 10 shekels = 83.33 g
1 Daric = 1/60 mina
1 quart = 0.97 litres
1 kur = 151.56 litres

Chronology of Persian Kings

Teispes	*c*.650-620
Cyrus I	*c*.620-590
Cambyses I	*c*.590-559
Cyrus II	559-530
Cambyses II	530-522
Bardiya	522
Darius I	522-486
Xerxes I	486-465
Artaxerxes I	465-424
Xerxes II	424 (45 days only)
Darius II (Ochus)	424-404
Artaxerxes II (Arsaces)	404-359
Artaxerxes III (Ochus)	359-338
Artaxerxes IV (Arses)	338-336
Darius III	336-330

Family Tree of the Persian Royal Family

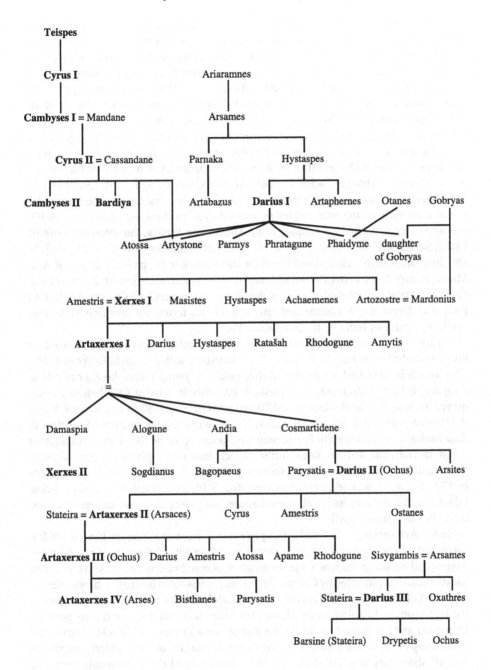

Brief Outline of the History of the Achaemenid Empire

In the mid-sixth century BC Cyrus II (the Great) conquered the ancient kingdoms of Media, Lydia, and Babylonia, as well as the eastern parts of ancient Iran in less than twenty years. He was the founder of the first Persian empire, which stretched from the eastern Mediterranean to India. His son and successor Cambyses II added Egypt in 525, completing the period of conquest and expansion. The lands of the empire were administered as satrapies, or provinces, headed by Persian nobles. After the death of Cambyses and his brother Bardiya, neither of whom had left any male offspring, Darius I succeeded to the throne in September 522, creating a royal dynasty called Achaemenid. The name derived from the eponymous founder of the empire, Achaemenes, whom Darius introduced as a common ancestor of both his family and that of Cyrus II. Though Darius I undertook an expedition against the Scythians in 518/7 and maintained control over the Aegean, his chief concern was the consolidation of the empire. In the course of the revolt of the Ionian cities, which began in 499/8, and which received limited support from Athens and Eretria, the satrapal centre of Lydia, Sardis, was burnt down. The revolt itself was completely suppressed by 493. In 490, in retaliation for Athens' and Eretria's interference in the political affairs of Asia Minor, an expedition under Datis and Artaphernes was sent out to punish the two Greek cities. Eretria was destroyed after a six-day siege, but in mainland Greece, the Persian force was defeated at Marathon and retreated. Darius turned his attention to the east and took control of India up to the River Indus.

Darius' son and successor Xerxes continued his father's policies and planned an invasion of the Greek mainland. But he first had to deal with a revolt in Egypt in 486/5, after which he installed his brother Achaemenes as satrap there. Another revolt in Babylon, led by Belšimanni, was quashed, probably in August 482, before Xerxes moved his army via the Hellespont and Thrace into Greece in 480, taking Athens. When the Persian fleet was defeated at Salamis, Xerxes withdrew the remains of his fleet to Asia Minor. Xerxes' return to Persia may have been forced by the outbreak of another revolt in Babylon, led by Šamaš-eriba, which had to be given priority. Though Mardonius together with an élite Persian army wintered in Thessaly and re-took Athens in 479, that army was so completely defeated at Plataea, Mardonius himself being killed, that the Persians had to abandon Greece; but failure there had no repercussions in the Persian empire itself.

Under Artaxerxes I (465-424), Egypt revolted from the Persian king in 464/3, supported by Athens, but was re-conquered in 454. In 450/49 the state of war between Athens and Persia ended when a peace treaty was concluded between Artaxerxes and an Athenian delegation led by Callias. Artaxerxes' designated heir to the throne, Xerxes (II), was killed after only 45 days on the throne, and, after a struggle for power between the half-brothers Sogdianus and Ochus, the latter succeeded to the throne between December and February 424, taking the throne name Darius II (424-404). Darius had been satrap of Hyrcania before he succeeded to the throne and was already married to his half-sister Parysatis. For the first time in the history of the Achaemenid dynasty a son, neither born of a Persian noblewoman, nor married to the daughter of one of the Persian noble families, succeeded to the throne. However, this did not weaken the royal dynasty.

Rivalry between the two sons of Darius II, Artaxerxes II (404-359) and Cyrus the Younger, led to a revolt by Cyrus, but his forces were defeated and he himself killed in 401. Under Artaxerxes II, who ruled for 46 years, the cults of the sun-god Mithra and the goddess of water and fertility, Anahita, were elevated to royal cults. After Artaxerxes' death in 359 and the murder of his designated heir to the throne, Darius, another son, Ochus, succeeded to the throne as Artaxerxes III. Though his reign was characterised in Greek sources as brutal, since he eliminated numerous members of his family in order to secure his power, Artaxerxes III's reign was marked by several important military successes. He quashed the revolt of Phoenician cities, led by Sidon, and in 343 re-conquered Egypt, which had revolted from Persia in 404 and then enjoyed 61 years of independence.

In a palace coup, the courtier Bagoas killed Artaxerxes III and put on the throne his only surviving son, Arses, who took the throne name Artaxerxes IV. Arses survived for only two years before being killed by Bagoas in 336. Bagoas replaced him with a distant member of the Achaemenid family, Artašata. As Darius III, the new king wisely rid himself of Bagoas and established himself on the Achaemenid throne. In Egypt, he quashed a revolt of Khababash, and possibly dealt successfully with a revolt in Babylon. With Alexander's arrival in 334, the Persian empire, for the first time in over 220 years, was faced with a foreign invasion. The Persian army was defeated at Issus in 333 and Gaugamela in 331. In 330 Alexander burnt the royal city of Persepolis. With the death of Darius III in the same year, the Achaemenid empire came to an end.

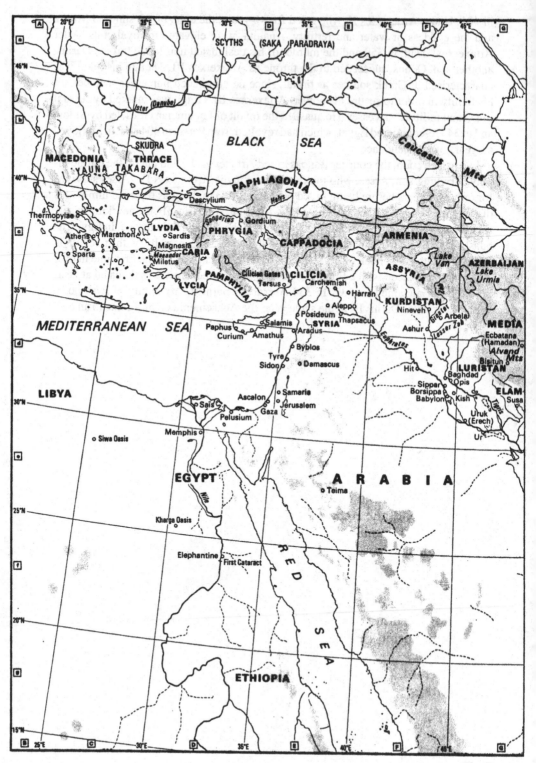

The Persian

CASPIAN SEA

ARAL SEA

KAZAKHSTAN

Jaxartes (Syr Darya)

MASSAGETAE

SAKA HAUMAVARGA

CHORASMIA

Oxus (Amu Darya)

SAKA TIGRAKHAUDA

Cyropolis

FERGHANA

SOGDIANA

Aï-Khanoum

Pamirs

Merv

MARGIANA

Balkh

BACTRIA

Mt. Demavand

HYRCANIA

Tehran

PARTHIA

ARIA

A F G H A N I S T A N

Hindu Kush

Peshawar

GANDARA

Himalayas

ZAGROS MTS

DRANGIANA

ARACHOSIA

PUNJAB

KHUZISTAN

Dahan-i Ghulaman

Kandahar

Multan

Anshan

Pasargadae

Persepolis

SEISTAN

Helmand

SATTAGYDIA?

Indus

PARSA

PERSIAN GULF

CARMANIA

INDIA

GEDROSIA

SIND

Land over 1,000 metres

SCALE

0   200   400   600   800   1000km

0   200   400   600miles

Empire

Part I. The Rise of Persia

Note A   The Near Eastern Sources

The primary sources for the study of the history of ancient Persia consist of documents of very different kinds. They include the royal chronicles written on the order of the kings of Babylon to record the events which occurred during their reign and the Persian royal inscriptions, written on the order of the Achaemenid kings. These inscriptions, which survive from the reign of Darius I to the reign of Artaxerxes III, were written as monolingual, bilingual or trilingual texts on stone tablets, carved into rocks and on walls of buildings, or incised on gold or silver sheets. Others were carved as minute inscriptions on the kings' seals. The principal scripts were Elamite, Babylonian and Old Persian. The last is a script invented by Darius I in order to record his own native language which was a dialect of Old Iranian that had never been written down before. The use of this 'royal script' was limited to the royal family and the Persian nobility surrounding the king, to identify a class of Persians who formed the élite at the Persian court. Both Elamite and Babylonian were scripts with a centuries-old scribal tradition in recording literary texts as well as administrative and legal documents in Elam, Assyria and Babylonia. The Persians adopted their administrative skills for their own bureaucracy, and Elamite and Babylonian were used for economic record-keeping as well as for official inscriptions. The Persian royal inscriptions offer an insight into the way the Persian kings wanted to be seen by their subjects and by the outside world. Beyond that, they reflect the way the Persian kings wanted their deeds to be regarded by posterity. The inscriptions range from building inscriptions, written to commemorate the building of a palace or some other royal or public monument, to historical accounts, exemplified in the great Inscription of Bisitun (**30, 35, 44**), the *res gestae* (record of achievement) of Darius I, commemorating his victory over Gaumata and his accession to the throne. For the Persian kings, their inscriptions had a timeless quality, preserving the memory of their kingship for eternity. It is for this reason that some of the building inscriptions, written on gold or silver sheets or on stone, were put beneath the palace floor, so that they could not be removed, unless through destruction. Minor royal inscriptions were written on artefacts crafted in the Achaemenid royal style and made of precious metal or stone.

No Near Eastern documents survive that throw light on the recruiting, training, or equipping of Persian infantry or cavalry, but we are abundantly informed about the working of the administration and economy of Persepolis by the clay tablets which were found at two places in this royal city, the building called the 'Treasury' and in a small office adjacent to the Fortification wall. Hence these clay tablets were called 'Treasury texts' and 'Fortification texts' respectively. These documents were written in Elamite cuneiform, reflecting the fact that the Persian administration adapted the bureaucracy of their predecessors. This is understandable if we consider that the Persians, who arrived in the region of Persis from around 1000 BC to settle alongside the indigenous Elamite population, were semi-nomadic, and although they may have had an oral tradition they had had no need for documents. The tablet texts deal with the transfer and issuing of foodstuffs for workers in Persepolis and the surrounding regions, accounting on a daily and monthly basis for their payments, which are made in kind (in the Fortification texts) and in silver (in the Treasury texts). Others record rations for members of the royal household, for administrators, for travellers, priests, workers and even animals. These texts are genuine sources, written for contemporary record-keeping, rather than to be kept for posterity; thus they were not written to serve any purpose other than being an immediate account of the daily proceedings of the Persian administration. As a source for the working population of Persis, for the activities of members of the royal family, for journeys across the empire undertaken by individuals visiting the king, for religious customs and the organisation of the administration as a whole, these documents are invaluable.

We have to see the economic documents from Babylonia in the same light. Babylonian administration remained intact after the Persian conquest, and as it was customary to date texts according to the regnal year of the king, Babylonian texts are sometimes our only means of documenting the reign of a Persian king with any accuracy.

Besides these three cuneiform scripts, Aramaic was widely used in the empire. In exceptional cases Aramaic was used in royal inscriptions, and it may have been used for royal correspondence. However, as Aramaic was mostly written on leather or parchment, relatively few texts have survived. Most spectacular perhaps is the correspondence of Arsames (**184**), the satrap of Egypt, whose letters to his steward in Egypt have survived, allowing a unique insight into events occurring on an estate owned by a member of the royal family. Another set of documents are the papyri and *ostraka* of the Jewish community from Egyptian Elephantine, where Jewish soldiers were stationed. Like the texts from Persepolis, the Aramaic documents are genuine primary sources written for the contemporary reader.

In Egypt itself, royal inscriptions carved on statues and stelae included hieroglyphic writing. Other texts were written in hieroglyphic or demotic only, without losing their official character.

A further source for the study of Persian history are the books of the Old Testament, especially *Kings*, *Chronicles*, *Esther* and *Nehemiah*. Though the historicity of these books must often be doubted, and though *Esther* was written at a later period, they give some insight into the way the Jewish community under the Persian kings wanted to be perceived. In particular, their view of Cyrus II as a Persian ruler well disposed towards the Jews lacks a historical perspective, and instead shows their uncritical reverence for Cyrus.

As becomes clear from the Near Eastern sources discussed above, the geographical distribution of the written documents is limited to the western part of the Persian empire, to Persia proper, Babylon, Egypt and Asia Minor. This is not to say that there were not any written records in the eastern part of the empire, but rather that due to the climate of the eastern provinces documents did not survive.

Note B   Herodotus' Contribution to Persian History

Born in Halicarnassus in Caria in *c*.484, Herodotus was a subject of the Persian king. His travels took him to Babylon and Egypt, where priests, tradesmen and interpreters supplied him with information about Persia. Thus, most of his information about Cambyses II was supplied to him by Egyptian priests. Likewise, stories of Egypt's revolt against Persia were still present in people's minds, and Herodotus himself refers to reminders of the revolt which he saw himself (**84**). In contrast to his travels to Babylon and Egypt, Herodotus visited neither the centre of the Persian empire nor its eastern provinces. He had no knowledge of the existence of the royal cities of Pasargadae and Persepolis. He obtained his information about Persian customs and Persian religion through oral sources, reflecting the oral tradition through which the history of a people had been predominantly transmitted in the Near East. The weakness of oral tradition is the problem of tracing the original source, its being subject to constant alterations, and the difficulty of verifying its truth through other accounts. It therefore had limited value and is sometimes erroneous. One example of the limits of oral accounts is Herodotus' passage on Persian religion. He is not familiar with the name of the principal god of the Achaemenids, Ahura Mazda, and instead refers to him as Zeus, while the god Mithra is regarded as a female deity (**199**). He regards the *magi* as a priesthood chiefly responsible for the sacrifices, which the Persepolis Fortification texts have shown to be wrong, since the *šatins*, the Persian priests, also poured libations for the gods (**192**). Not being able to read cuneiform or speak other languages, Herodotus was dependent on translations of official or semi-official documents into Greek from Old Persian or Aramaic, or on information provided by Greek and Persian tradesmen, workers, interpreters and informants who had lived in or had travelled to Persia. Among those who might have passed on information to Herodotus were the exiled Spartan king Demaratus (Hdt.6.70.2), the Athenian exile Dicaeus (Hdt.8.65.1), or the Persian Zopyrus, son of Megabyxus (2), who fled from Persia some time between the late 440s and early 420s (**85**).

Despite his limitations, Herodotus provides a wealth of information about the Persian nobility and the peoples of the empire. He has a remarkable knowledge of the events concerning the revolt of Gaumata/Smerdis and Darius' accession to the throne. Herodotus did not have first-hand knowledge of the Inscription of Bisitun; nevertheless the story of the seven Persian nobles must have circulated within the Persian empire and survived for almost a century before Herodotus wrote down his version of the events of 522. With the exception of Aspathines' name, he accurately records the names of the Persian nobles involved in the conspiracy. While his substituting for the name of Ardumaniš that of Aspathines can be explained by Ardumaniš's death, the name of Otanes' father, Pharnaspes, cannot be reconciled with the name given in the Bisitun Inscription, Thukra (**44**). However, he makes no comment on Darius' claim to be the legitimate heir to the throne, but rather regards him as an Achaemenid, a much disputed issue in Achaemenid history. Moral standards set up in the royal inscriptions (**103, 104**), such as telling the truth, being a good horseman and good bowman, are reflected in Herodotus' own words (**105**). The king's appreciation of numerous offspring, referred to in Herodotus, is known from the Bisitun Inscription and the Fortification texts, which grant special rations to mothers (**157, 158**).

Many names which occur in Herodotus have been identified as Greek renderings of Persian names. Among the members of the royal family are Darius' wife Artystone, reflecting the Elamite name Irtašduna, and Pharnakes, the uncle of Darius I, who is known from the Fortification texts as Parnaka. Darius' brother Artaphernes, who was satrap of Sardis between 511 and 492, appears in the Persepolis Fortification texts as Irdapirna (**189**). Likewise, the Persian noble Gobryas appears in the royal inscriptions (**44, 112**) and the Fortification texts (**169**), as well as his son Mardonius (**168**). The name Tithaeus (Hdt.7.88.1) is probably the Greek rendering of Ziššawiš (**144-146**), and Datis the Mede (Hdt.6.94.2) has been identified with Datiya (**56**).

Herodotus' familiarity with the administration of the Persian empire is reflected in his use of the term 'satrapies', which is adopted into the Greek language. His list of the lands of the Persian empire is testimony to the remarkable achievement of the *Histories*. This list, which reflects a detailed knowledge of the names of the peoples of the empire, and his list of the contingents of Xerxes' army indicate that Herodotus must have drawn his information from official or semi-official sources translated into Greek which might have been available to him in Halicarnassus. The accuracy of Herodotus' information is reflected in the names of the commanders, many of which can be verified through the Persepolis Fortification texts. Other cases show the limits of his knowledge. Although Darius I undertook a reform of the tribute payments, it is clear from Near Eastern and Greek sources that the collection of tribute had already been introduced by Cyrus II, and was not an innovation of Darius I. The Persepolis Fortification texts furthermore have proved that, contrary to Herodotus' view, Persis was not exempt from paying taxes.

Herodotus' description of the Royal Road leading from Sardis to Susa shows that he possessed some information on the post-stations and the messenger services which operated throughout the empire.

1.1 CYRUS I
The seal and inscription of Cyrus
1   Cyrus of Anshan, son of Teispes.

PFS 93

1. Impression of Cyrus' seal

The inscription of the seal belonging to Cyrus I is impressed on clay tablets from Persepolis. This is the earliest written evidence for a Persian king. It identifies Cyrus I (Elam. *Kuraš*), the grandfather of Cyrus II (the Great), as the ruler of the city of Anshan in Parsa (modern Fars), and also documents the name of his father, Teispes (Elam. *Zišpiš*), who is the oldest known member of the Persian royal family. While the seal inscriptions of Darius I and his successors are written either in Old Persian only or in three scripts (Elamite, Babylonian, Old Persian), the inscription of Cyrus I is written in Elamite. The scene depicted on the seal is crafted in the artistic style of the Neo-Elamite period. It shows a man on horseback (perhaps Cyrus?) pursuing his enemies with a spear, while two slain adversaries lie beneath the horse. By using Elamite script and imagery, Cyrus I expresses his affinity with Elam, the kingdom which had ruled in Fars and Susiana until

Susa was destroyed by the Assyrians in 646, and under whose rule Persian peoples had settled peacefully in Fars from the beginning of the first millennium BC onwards. It is remarkable that the seal of Cyrus I continued to be used in the administration of Darius I.

1.2. The Inscriptions of Ariaramnes and Arsames
Inscription of Ariaramnes from Hamadan

2 §1. Ariaramnes, the Great King, king of kings, king of (*lit. in*) Persia, son of Teispes the king, grandson of Achaemenes. §2. Ariaramnes the king says: 'The great god Ahura Mazda has bestowed upon me this country of Persia, which I hold, and which possesses good horses and good men. By the favour of Ahura Mazda, I am king of this country.' §3. Ariaramnes the king says: 'May Ahura Mazda bring me aid.'

AmH

Inscription of Arsames from Hamadan

3 §1. Arsames, the Great King, king of kings, king of (*lit. in*) Persia, son of Ariaramnes the king, the Achaemenid. §2. Arsames the king says: 'Ahura Mazda, the great god, the greatest of gods, made me king. He bestowed upon me the country of Persia, with good men and good horses. By the favour of Ahura Mazda, I hold this land. May Ahura Mazda protect me and my royal house, and may he protect this country which I hold.'

AsH

Both inscriptions were written in Old Persian on gold tablets and were allegedly found in Ecbatana, the former capital of the kingdom of Media and a royal residence of the Persian kings. Today the city, which is situated in northwestern Iran, is called Hamadan. The style of the inscription follows that of the royal inscriptions of Darius I, Xerxes, and Artaxerxes I (see below **Part II**): Ariaramnes and Arsames bear royal titles and invoke the support of the principal Persian god Ahura Mazda (see below **191-194**). However, several facts cast doubt on the historicity of these two inscriptions: the grammatical errors made in the Old Persian language and the lack of logograms, signs, which are to be read as a whole word. The fact that these gold tablets came from an uncontrolled excavation adds to the problems. As it is accepted in scholarship that neither Ariaramnes nor Arsames was king of Persia, and that the form of writing, Old Persian, was a new script first used by Darius I (see DB IV: §70, **44**), modern scholarship doubts the historicity of these texts. Alternatively, they could have been written by Darius I himself in support of his kingship. For Darius' claim that Ariaramnes and Arsames were his royal predecessors see **44**.

1.3. Cyrus II
Cyrus' inscription from Pasargadae, in the plain of Murghab

4 I am Cyrus the King, an Achaemenid.

CMa

In this inscription found in two copies in the Audience Hall and the Residential Palace in Pasargadae, the royal residence of Cyrus II, Cyrus is identified as an Achaemenid. This titulature stands in contrast to Cyrus' royal title given in the Nabonidus Chronicle (see below **11**) and in the Cyrus Cylinder (see below **12**), in which the king is referred to as 'king of Anshan' or 'king of Parsa'. Because the inscription is written in Elamite, Babylonian and Old Persian, the script invented by Darius I (DB IV: §70, **44**), the inscription has to be dated after the reign of Cyrus II. It was possibly set up by Darius I himself.

The Persian tribes

5 [125.3] There are many tribes of Persians, and Cyrus united some of them and persuaded them to rebel against the Medes. These tribes, on which all other Persians depend, were the Pasargadae, the Maraphians and the Maspians. The Pasargadae are the noblest of these, and to them belongs the clan of the

Achaemenids, from which the Persian kings descend. The other Persians are these: the Panthialaeans, the Derusians, and the Germanians, who are engaged in husbandry, while the others, the Daans, the Mardians, the Dropicans, and the Sagartians, are nomads.

Herodotus 1.125.3

A distinction is being made between three different social classes, the nobility, the peasants, and the nomadic peoples of Persia. Cyrus II and his ancestors probably belonged to the noble clan of the Pasargadae. 'Pasargadae' has been explained to mean 'those who wield strong clubs'. It was also the name given to the first royal city built by Cyrus II in the plain of Murghab in Fars in the southwest of modern Iran (see above **4** and below **109**). It is the Greek rendering of a place name which is Batrakataš in Elamite. (For the notion that Cyrus II descended from the nomadic tribe of the Mardians see below **9**.) Herodotus follows the view that the royal house of the Achaemenids stemmed from the Pasargadae and had already existed at the time of Cyrus II. But it is more likely that we need to distinguish between the early Persian kings from Teispes to Cambyses II and Bardiya and the royal clan of the Achaemenids beginning with the reign of Darius I. (For further discussion of the Achaemenids see below, p.31.). Little, if anything, is known about the other tribes mentioned in this passage. It is probable that a division between settled and nomadic Persian tribes existed.

The upbringing of Cyrus

6   [107.1] He (*Astyages, king of Media*) had a daughter, whom he called Mandane. About her he dreamt that such a stream of water flowed from her that it filled his city and overflowed the whole of Asia. He told his dream to those *magi* (*Persian priests*) who interpreted dreams, and when he heard each point explained, he was terrified. [107.2] Therefore, when Mandane was of marriageable age, he would not give her in marriage to any of the Medes of suitable rank, in case the dream should come true, but married her to a Persian named Cambyses (*I*), a man whom he knew to be well born and of a quiet temper; for Astyages regarded Cambyses as being of much lower rank than a Mede of middle standing.

Herodotus 1.107.1–2

In Herodotus' version of Cyrus' rise to power, the Persian king was identified as a grandson of the Median king. The story of the marriage between Cambyses I and Astyages' daughter Mandane was probably circulated after Cyrus' conquest of Media in 547, and served to legitimate Cyrus' rule over Media. According to Herodotus (**13**), Cyrus revolted against Media in order to end Astyages' overlordship over Parsa. While Near Eastern archaeological and written sources confirm that Parsa was a small principality in the sixth century BC, we have no proof that it was in any way dependent on Media at that time (**11** II:1-4). The *magi* were a group of priests known only from western Iran (see below pp.90f.).

7   [2.1] It is said that the father of Cyrus (*II*) was Cambyses (*I*), king of Persia. This Cambyses belonged to the tribe of the Persidae; the Persidae take their name from Perseus. It is agreed that his mother was Mandane, the daughter of Astyages, the king of the Medes.

Xenophon, *Cyropaedia* 1.2.1

This highly inaccurate statement on the origin of the name for the Persians reflects a hellenocentric view. The Persians took their name from the region of Parsa, where they had lived for several centuries alongside the indigenous Elamite population. Xenophon follows Herodotus in confirming the marriage alliance between Cambyses I and the daughter of Astyages, but does not provide an explanation of the political relationship between Media and Persia.

8   [4.7] Harpagus was afraid that if the throne should pass to the king's daughter when Astyages died (for he had produced no male heir), then she, unable to avenge the infant's death by taking action against her father, would do so by punishing his henchman. Accordingly he handed the boy over to the herdsman of the king's cattle to be exposed. [4.8] It so happened that at the same time a son had been born to the herdsman also, [4.9] and when his wife heard of the order for exposure of the royal child, she earnestly begged that the boy be brought and shown to her. [4.10] Worn out by her entreaties, the herdsman returned to the wood to find a bitch at the infant's side offering the child her teats and keeping away wild animals and birds.

Justin 1.4.7-10 (transl. J.C. Yardley)

The story of the Mede Harpagus, who had been ordered by Astyages to kill the infant Cyrus, but disobeyed his order and instead entrusted the child to a cowherd and his wife, is recorded at length in Herodotus (1.108-130). Justin echoes Herodotus' version of the humble upbringing of Cyrus, the exposure of the infant and subsequent adoption by the king's herdsman and his wife.

9   [66.2] A law existed among the Medes that any man who was poor could go to a wealthy man and put himself into his care in order to be supported, so that he might be properly fed and clothed, and according to the custom was this man's slave. (...) [66.3] Now there was a young man called Cyrus, a Mardian, who approached a royal servant who was in charge of beautifying the royal estate. This Cyrus was the son of Atradates, who, out of poverty, had become a brigand; his wife, called Argoste, the mother of Cyrus, herded goats. [66.4] In order to be reared by this man, Cyrus offered himself into his care, and he beautified the royal garden and was very careful about his task. His supervisor therefore gave him a better set of clothes and took him from the group that worked outdoors to the one which worked inside, right near the king (...). [66.5] Having distinguished himself in these matters, he (*Cyrus*) went to Artembares, who was in charge of the cupbearers and himself handed the drinking cup to the king. He warmly accepted him, and appointed him cupbearer to those who dined at the same table as the king.

Nicolaus of Damascus *FGrH* 90 F 66.2-5

According to Nicolaus of Damascus, Cyrus belonged to one of the lowest tribes of Persia, the Mardians, and became a servant of the Median king, first looking after the royal gardens, and eventually becoming the king's cupbearer. The story of Cyrus' upbringing, which is a version of the tale of the humble origins of a noble-spirited king, can be traced back to the story of the Assyrian king Sargon of Akkad (2334-2279). In this story, Sargon was described as the child of non-royal parents. The infant Sargon was placed in a reed basket, which flowed down the Euphrates river. Akki, a drawer of water, rescued Sargon, reared and trained him as a gardener, but eventually Sargon was proclaimed king of the city of Akkad. The story of Moses provides another variation of the tale, whose purpose was to convey the image of the morally good leader, whose noble manner was rooted in his spirit and not in his upbringing. The historical value of these stories is very doubtful, but their ideological importance has to be acknowledged.

10   He (*Ctesias*) speaks thus immediately about Astyages, to whom Cyrus was not related (...). He (*Astyages*) was freed not much later by Cyrus himself and was honoured like a father; and his daughter Amytis at first received the respect of a mother, but was then given to Cyrus as his wife.

Ctesias *FGrH* 688 F1

According to Ctesias' story, Cyrus was not related to Astyages before his conquest of Media. He married a daughter of the king, called Amytis, and regarded Astyages as his father. Such a 'political adoption' was a common occurrence in the ancient Near East, supporting the conqueror's political claim to succeed to the kingship of the deposed king. The marriage of the defeated king's daughter to the victorious king sealed the political treaty concluded between the two parties, and served to legitimate the conqueror's succession to the throne (see also below **176-180**).

The conquests of Cyrus
The Nabonidus Chronicle

The text of the so-called Nabonidus Chronicle is written in Neo-Babylonian cuneiform on one clay tablet, which now is in the British Museum, London (BM 35382). Cuneiform scripts were used in the Near East from the fourth millennium BC onwards. The wedge-shaped signs were inscribed on clay tablets using a rectangular-ended instrument. Economic and administrative texts as well as chronicles recording the achievements of the Near Eastern kings and literary texts were written in cuneiform scripts. The Nabonidus Chronicle, the official record of the reign of Nabonidus (555-539), documents the events beginning with the accession of the last Babylonian king, and ending with the conquest of Babylon by Cyrus II in 539. Despite the lacunae and occasional illegibility of the text, the chronicle is a vital primary source for the beginning of Persian rule, since it refers to Cyrus' conquests of Media, possibly Lydia, and Babylon. The text was first published in 1882.

11   Column II

[1] (Astyages) mustered (his army) and marched against Cyrus (Bab. *Kuraš*), king of Anshan, for conquest [...]. [2] The army mutinied against Astyages (Bab. *Ištumegu*) and he was taken prisoner. Th[ey handed him over?] to Cyrus [...]. [3] Cyrus marched to Ecbatana, the royal city. Silver, gold, goods, property, [...], [4] which he carried off as booty (from) Ecbatana, he took to Anshan. The goods (and) treasures of the army of [...]. (...) [10] The ninth year: Nabonidus, the king (was) in Tema, (while) the prince, the officers, (and) the army (were) in Akkad.(...).[15] In the month Nisannu (*March/April*) Cyrus, king of Parsu, mustered his army and [16] crossed the Tigris below Arbela. In the month Ayyaru (*April/May*) (he marched) to Ly[dia?]. [17] He defeated its king, took its possessions, (and) stationed his own garrison (there) [...]. [18] Afterwards the king and his garrison was in it [...]. (...)

Column III

(...)[12-13] In the month Tašritu (*September/October*) when Cyrus did battle at Opis on the (bank of?) the Tigris against the army of Akkad, the people of Akkad [14] retreated. He carried off the plunder (and) slaughtered the people. On the fourteenth day Sippar was captured without a battle. [15] Nabonidus fled. On the sixteenth day (*12 October 539*) Ugbaru, governor of the Guti, and the army of Cyrus [16-17] entered Babylon without a battle. Afterwards, after Nabonidus had retreated, he was captured in Babylon. Until the end of the month the shield-(bearing troops) of the Guti surrounded the gates of Esagil. (But) [18-19] there was no interruption (of rites) in Esagil or the (other) temples and no date (for a performance) was missed. On the third day of the month Arahšamnu (*29 October 539*) Cyrus entered Babylon. [...] were filled with [...] before him. There was peace in the city while Cyrus [20] spoke (his) greeting to all of Babylon. Gobryas (Bab. *Gubaru*), his governor (Bab. *pihātu*), appointed the district officers in Babylon. [21] From the month Kislimu (*November/December*) to the month Addaru (*February/March*) the gods of Akkad which Nabonidus had brought down to Babylon [22] returned to their places. On the night of the eleventh of the month of Arahšamnu Ugbaru died. In the month [...] [23] the king's wife died. From the twenty-seventh of the month of Addaru to the third of the month Nisannu [there was] (an official) mourning period in Akkad. [24] All of the people bared their heads. On the fourth day, when Cambyses (Bab. *Kambuzija*), son of C[yrus], [25-26] went to Egidrikalammasummu the [...]-official of Nabu who [...]. When he came, because of the Elamite [...] the hand of Nabu [...] [27] spears and quivers from [...] crown prince to the wo[rk...]. [28] [...] Nabu to Esagil [...] before Bel and the son of B[el...].(...)

adapted from Grayson, 1975: no.7

Column II

[1] Astyages, king of Media 585-550. The Babylonian chronicle dates the battle between Astyages and Cyrus to the sixth year of Nabonidus' reign, which is 550/549. According to the chronicle Astyages fought an offensive battle against Cyrus, aiming to conquer the Persian realm. The mutiny of Astyages' army seems to have been the decisive factor for Cyrus' victory. The chronicle neither refers to a familial relationship between Astyages and Cyrus, nor to an overlordship of the Median king over Persia. The site of the battle has traditionally been located in the plain of Murghab in Fars, and it is thought that Cyrus built the city of Pasargadae on the site to commemorate his victory (see above **4** and below **17, 109**).

Cyrus, king of Anshan (559-530): The title of the early Persian kings as 'king of Anshan' originates in the royal title of the kings of Elam, 'king of Anshan and Susa'. The kingdom of Elam existed for about 3,000 years and had been ruled by two cities, Anshan in Fars, and Susa in southwest Iran. When the city of Susa was destroyed by the Assyrians in 646, Elamite power finally came to an end, and a local principality arose in Parsu/Parsa under Teispes and his son Cyrus I. In adopting the Elamite royal title, Cyrus regards himself as the successor to the kings of Elam (see below **94-102**; see also **1**).

[3-4] The conquest of Media was completed when Cyrus took the Median capital Ecbatana. The city remained a royal residence of the Persian kings throughout Achaemenid rule (see below **109**).

[10] The ninth year = 547/6. The city of Tema or Taima is located in northwest Arabia. Akkad was the name of a city founded by Sargon, possibly built in the south Mesopotamian plain, but it has not yet been located. In later periods the name was extended to refer to a region, possibly the area between Baghdad and Nippur. The term 'Akkadian', which refers to the cuneiform writing of the Old, Middle, and Neo-Babylonian periods, also is derived from the name of this city.

[15] In the month Nisannu = March/April 547/6. Cyrus, king of Parsu: Parsu, or Parsa, is a reference to the region which the Persians inhabited. From the beginning of the first millennium BC onwards Persian tribes had migrated to this area from the north and northwest, and in a process of acculturation, had lived alongside the indigenous population. From Parsu/Parsa derives the name later given to the whole of the empire, as well as to the people themselves. The title 'king of Parsu' is used here as an alternative to the title 'king of Anshan' in Col.II:1, referring to the principality rather than the city (for Cyrus' title see below **12**, Cyrus Cylinder: 1.21).

[16-18] In the month Ayyaru = April/May 547/6. The Babylonian chronicle reports a further campaign of Cyrus' army against a country. Unfortunately the text is illegible here and does not allow a clear identification of the place, though traditionally it has been identified with Lydia, which Cyrus conquered in the early 540s. The city of Arbela is situated in northern Mesopotamia. With Cyrus' conquest of Babylonia, this former Assyrian city was now incorporated into the Persian empire, and was probably the capital city of the satrapy of Assyria (see DB I: §6, **44**). For an explanation of the term 'satrapy' see below **123-127**.

Column III

[12-14] In the month Tašritu = September/October 539. Following the conquest of Media and Lydia, Cyrus led his third military campaign against Babylonia. His first battle against the city of Opis, east of the Tigris river, decided the fate of Babylonia. The chronicle records the brutality of Cyrus' attack, during which the population of Opis was massacred and the city plundered by Cyrus' army.

[15-19] After the Babylonian defeat at Opis, both Sippar and Babylon surrendered, opening the gates of their cities to the enemy. In doing so, the people of Sippar and Babylon had made a choice between accepting a new ruler or being killed and having their city destroyed. The chronicle clearly depicts Cyrus as a ruthless military conqueror, a portrait which stands in sharp contrast to the image of the benign ruler related by himself (see below **12**), and presented in books of the Old Testament (see below **201-204**).

The Babylonian king Nabonidus had tried to escape, but was captured by the Persians several days later in Babylon. He possibly spent the rest of his life on an estate in Carmania (Berossus *FGrH* 680 F9).

Esagil: the temple of the god Bel-Marduk in Babylon. Cyrus' army was supported by the army of Ugbaru, governor of Gutium, the region north of the city of Opis. The soldiers were immediately put in charge of maintaining peace in the city. Most notable is the concern for the continuation of the religious festival in the temple of Bel-Marduk.

Arahšamnu = October/November 539: Cyrus entered the city only *after* matters had been settled by Ugbaru. The city had surrendered, the Persian army had been installed in the city, Nabonidus had been taken pris-

oner and the religious ceremonies continued. Cyrus now entered the city in an official ceremony, presenting himself to the people of Babylon as the new king.

[20-22] Gobryas/Gubaru (different from the Persian noble who held high office under Darius I): Cyrus
appointed him governor of Babylon. As the official in charge, he appointed the local administrators for the
satrapy of Babylonia. Babylonian texts document that he governed until 28 August 525.

Casting himself as the benign ruler, Cyrus spent the next four months, from Kislimu (*November/
December*) to Addaru (*February/March*), restoring the religious cults of Babylon (see **12**). Nabonidus was
accused of having neglected the Babylonian gods in favour of the moon-god Sin, whom he worshipped in
Harran, in northern Babylonia.

Cyrus' policy of 'religious tolerance' was introduced to ensure broad popular support. By allowing the
continuation of local religious cults and customs, Persian kings signalled to the people that their co-operation was rewarded with a degree of continuation of their lifestyle. Resistance to Persian rule, on the other
hand, was severely punished. This policy also aided Cyrus' collaboration with the local élite, which was
given official tasks under the new king.

[23-28] The king's wife: Though not entirely clear, this may be a reference to the death of Cyrus' wife,
whose name is known from Herodotus (2.1; 3.2.2; see below **176**) as Cassandane. She may well have accompanied the king on his campaign as a member of the royal entourage. The official mourning period proclaimed
for her lasted from February/March 539 to 23 March 538 and followed the traditional ceremony, during
which the people of Babylonia, as a sign of mourning, bared their heads.

Cambyses II, the son of Cyrus II and Cassandane, was installed as co-regent in Babylon in an official ceremony. This co-regency lasted for only one year, 538/7, and is a unique occurrence in the history of Persian
kingship.

The Cyrus Cylinder

12   [...] [5] He (*Nabonidus*) made an imitation of Esagila [...] to Ur and the other cult
centres. [6] He introduced a cult order for them which was unsuitable [...], and in
malice [7] stopped regular sacrifice. The worship of Marduk, king of the gods, he
removed from his heart. [8] While he pursued the downfall of his (*Marduk's*) city,
[...] daily [...] he destroyed his (people) with a merciless yoke. [9] In response to
their lament the Enlil of the gods (*Marduk*) raged with wrath [...] their area. The
gods who lived in them left their dwelling-places. [10] To his (*Marduk's*) anger
he brought them into Babylon. Marduk [....], (however), turned to all the
places whose residences had been left, [11] and to the people of Sumer and Akkad,
who had become like corpses [...], he was compassionate. He critically examined
all the countries, and [12] searched for a just ruler who suited his heart. He took
Cyrus, king of Anshan, by the hand, proclaimed his nomination, called his name
for the lordship over the whole world. [13] He made Gutium and all the
Ummanmanda (*the Medes*) subject to him. While he cared for the black-headed
people whom he (*Marduk*) had allowed into his (*Cyrus'*) hands [14] in justice and
righteousness, Marduk, the great lord, the protector of his people, looked at his
(*Cyrus'*) good deeds and his righteous heart with pleasure. [15] He (*Marduk*)
commanded him (*Cyrus*) to go to Babylon, and let him take the road to Babylon.
Like a friend and companion he walked by his side, [16] while his extensive
troops, whose number was immeasurable like the water of a river, marched at his
side, with their weapons fastened. [17] Without battle and fighting he let him enter
Babylon. He saved his (*Marduk's*) city Babylon from its oppression; he handed
over to him Nabonidus, the king who did not revere him. [18] All the people
of Babylon, the whole of the land of Sumer and Akkad, princes and governors
knelt before him, kissed his feet, rejoiced at his kingship. Their faces shone.
[19] The lord, who through his help has revived the gods (?), who spared them
disaster and oppression, they praised again and again in gratitude, honoured his
name.

[20] I, Cyrus, king of the world, great king, mighty king, king of Babylon, king of Sumer and Akkad, king of the four quarters (of the world), [21] son of Cambyses (*I*), great king, king of Anshan, grandson of Cyrus (I), great king, king of Anshan, great-grandson of Teispes, great king, king of Anshan, [22] eternal seed of kingship, whose reign was loved by Bel(-Marduk) and Nabu, and whose kingship they wanted to rejoice in their hearts, when I had entered Babylon peacefully, [23] I began, with (the people's) acclamation and rejoicing, my rule in the palace. Marduk, the great lord, had won my great heart, which Babylon [...], and daily I showed my reverence for him, [24] while my extensive troops marched peacefully through Babylon. In the whole land of Sumer and Akkad I did not allow any troublemaker to arise. [25] His city of Babylon and all his cult-centres I maintained in prosperity. The [...] people of Babylon, who, against the will of the gods [...] (had suffered) a yoke unsuitable for them [through that man (*Nabonidus*)], [26] I offered relief from their exhaustion, and ended their servitude. Marduk, the great lord, rejoiced at (my good) deeds, and [27] he blessed me, Cyrus, the king, who reveres him, Cambyses, (my) son, the offspring of my loins, and all my troops, [28] and we walked before him in well-being. (On his) sublime (command), all the kings of the entire world, who are enthroned, [29] of the corners of the world, from the Upper to the Lower Sea, those who live in (faraway lands), the kings of the lands of Amurru, who live in tents, brought [30] their considerable tribute and kissed my feet in Babylon. From (Nineveh), Assur and Susa, [31] from Akkad, Ešunna, Zamban, Meturnu, and Der, to the land of Gutium, the cult places on the other side of the Tigris, whose sanctuaries had been deserted a long time ago, [32] I returned (their) gods to their (rightful) place, and let them be housed there forever. I gathered all their former inhabitants and returned them to their houses, [33] and the gods of Sumer and Akkad, whom Nabonidus had brought into Babylon to the wrath of the great lord (*Marduk*), I installed, on the command of Marduk, the great lord, [34] in their sanctuaries as a place of heart's joy. May all the gods whom I returned to their cult places [35] speak every day to Bel(-Marduk) and Nabu for my long life, speak in my favour and say to Marduk, my lord: 'Cyrus, the king who reveres you, and Cambyses, his son [36] [...]. They may be (rulers of the black-headed people until the days [...]?).' All lands lived in peace. [37] [...] a goose, two ducks, and ten (fat) pigeons beyond the regular goose, ducks and (fat) pigeons [38] [...] I increased. The wall Imgur-Illil, the great wall of Babylon, I strove to strengthen and [39] [...]. The quay wall made of baked brick at the bank of the moat which an earlier king had (built and not completed), whose (incomplete) construction [40] (therefore had not surrounded the city), [...] on the outside, which no previous king had done, his (building-)troops, the contingent (of his land) in Babylon. [41][...] I built [with asphalt] and baked bricks again and (completed) its (construction). [42] [...] (I adorned her wide gates) [...] (gates made of cedar wood) with bronze fittings, thresholds and stops (made of copper). (Where the gates were [43] I put up) [...] An inscription of Aššurbanipal, a king who ruled before me, (which I saw inside) [44] [...] [45] [...] forever [...].

adapted from Berger 1975:192–234

The text is written in Akkadian on a barrel-shaped clay cylinder. It was found in Babylon in 1879, and is now in the British Museum, London (BM 90920). No other inscription of the Persian period has been written on this shape; it had mainly been used by Assyrian and Babylonian kings for building inscriptions. Cyrus chose this shape deliberately to link himself to his royal (Assyrian) predecessors, and at the same time added a subtle touch to his attempt to legitimise his kingship in Babylonia. This link is further confirmed by his reference to an old inscription of Aššurbanipal, king of Assyria (668-?631), which Cyrus put up near the entrance gates of the city. In describing Aššurbanipal as his 'predecessor' Cyrus wanted to be seen as a successor of the Assyrian king, and not as a foreign conqueror.

The text of the Cyrus Cylinder was written by a Babylonian priest or a royal scribe on the orders of Cyrus II after his conquest of Babylon in 539 and consists of two parts. The first part (§§1-19) gives a negative account of the rule of Nabonidus and relates the story of Cyrus' support of the Babylonian god Marduk, the city god of Babylon, in his conquest of Babylon. In the second part (§§20-45), written in the first person singular, Cyrus relates his 'peaceful' conquest of Babylon and expresses his reverence for the Babylonian god Marduk. Cyrus' Babylonian conquest is described as a divine intervention which ends the sacrilegious deeds of Nabonidus, who is accused of having neglected the cult of Marduk in favour of other cults. With this divine sanctioning, Cyrus marched towards Babylon and his army took the city without giving battle; he was welcomed by the people of Babylon as a saviour.

The second part begins with the royal title and Cyrus' genealogy. Cyrus refers to himself as 'king of the world, ... king of Babylon, ... king of the four quarters', the last title being a reference to the four corners of the world. He then adds his own royal title, 'king of Anshan', including a list of his royal ancestors, his father Cambyses I, his grandfather Cyrus I and his great-grandfather Teispes, who were all kings of Anshan. Emphasising that he enjoyed the support of the Babylonian gods, Bel, which is another name for the god Marduk, and Nabu, the god of writing and wisdom, he describes his peaceful entrance into the city of Babylon. Cyrus puts himself in charge of the religious cult ceremonies of Babylon, thus presenting himself as the benign ruler with considerable religious tolerance. He restores the cult centres of the gods of Babylon, and the people who worship these gods are allowed to return to these places. Similarly, a document comparable to the Cyrus Cylinder, found in the city of Ur, and probably to be dated to the time of Cyrus, refers to the rebuilding of the Moon-temple of Ur. This evidence may indicate that Cyrus intended to associate himself with the principal deity of each conquered city, ordering the restoration of temples and ensuring the continuation of their cult ceremonies. Such actions reflect Cyrus' political motivation for the restoration of local cults rather than his devotion to a particular god.

Cyrus' depiction of himself as peaceful conqueror, who enjoyed the support of the Babylonian god Marduk, and who met with no opposition when taking Babylon, is a 'touched-up' version of the actual events. The Babylonian report of the massacre at Opis (see **11**:III,12-14) stands in sharp contrast to the glossy image of Cyrus' account. Cyrus' seeming reverence for the Babylonian god Marduk was in fact a political stratagem to show him as a restorer, and not as a conqueror, of Babylon.

Greek evidence for Cyrus' campaigns

13 [127.1] Now that the Persians had found a leader, they were eager to win their freedom, since they had resented being ruled by the Medes for a long time. When Astyages learned about Cyrus' actions, he sent a messenger to summon him. [127.2] But Cyrus told the messenger to report that Astyages would see him sooner than he wished. Hearing this, Astyages provided all the Medes with weapons, and, as if he had lost his senses and forgotten how he had treated him, appointed Harpagus as their general. [127.3] Thus, when the Medes marched out to meet the Persians in battle, they deserted to the Persian side, and only those who were not in the know, fought; most of them played the coward and fled.

Herodotus 1.127

Under the leadership of Cyrus, the Persians decided to end Astyages' control over their country. While it cannot be confirmed that the Median king did in fact control Persia, the Nabonidus Chronicle records the mutiny of the Median army (see **11**:II,2).

14 [53.1] Croesus ordered the Lydians who were to deliver the gifts to the temples (*of Apollo at Delphi and Amphiaraus at Oropus*) to ask the oracles whether he should campaign against the Persians, and whether he should win over an ally. [53.2] When the Lydians arrived at the places they had been sent to, they presented their gifts and asked the oracles: 'Croesus, king of Lydia and other peoples, believing that these are the only true oracles among men, has sent you such presents as are due to you, and now inquires of you whether he should campaign against the Persians, and whether he should win over an ally.' [53.3] This is what they asked, and both oracles replied in the same way, prophesying that if Croesus attacked the Persians, he would destroy a great empire. They also advised that he should find out who were the most powerful of the Greeks and make an alliance with them.

Herodotus 1.53

Following the fall of the Median empire, Croesus of Lydia prepared for a battle against Cyrus, first marching into Cappadocia, where he took the fortress of Pteria (Boğazköy?). This campaign possibly served to enlarge his own realm (see Hdt.1.73.1, 75.3). He had earlier sent messengers to the oracle of Delphi (and other Greek oracles (Hdt.1.46.2)) and the oracle of Ammon in Libya (Hdt.1.46.3). The irony of the identical prophecy of Delphi and Oropus is that Croesus misinterpreted the message, and in what became a classic case of *hybris* took their view as proof of his invincibility if he fought against the Persians. Croesus found allies in the Spartans, Babylonians and Egyptians (Hdt.1.77.2).

15   [86.1] So the Persians took Sardis and made Croesus himself a prisoner, after he had reigned fourteen years and been besieged fourteen days, and, as the oracle had prophesied, he had destroyed a mighty empire - his own.

Herodotus 1.86.1

The Lydian capital Sardis was taken in 547, causing the collapse of the Lydian empire. Croesus, the last king, had ruled from c.561/0 to 547/6. As Herodotus relates (1.86.2-6), Croesus was rescued from burning on the pyre by the benign Cyrus and taken to Ecbatana. The scene depicting Croesus on the pyre is beautifully imagined on an Athenian vase from Vulci in Etruria, dated to the early fifth century and attributed to the painter Myson. Presentation of historical events is rare in Greek art, and the fact that this scene is depicted here reflects the impact of the fall of the Lydian empire on the Mediterranean world. The vase is now in the Louvre Museum in Paris.

16   [153.3] He (*Cyrus*) entrusted Sardis to Tabalus, a Persian, and put Pactyes, a Lydian, in charge of Croesus' gold and that of the other Lydians, while he himself returned to Ecbatana, taking Croesus with him, not regarding the Ionians as important enough to give them priority. [153.4] He wanted to campaign in person against Babylon and the Bactrians, as well as the Scythians and the Egyptians. He therefore determined to assign to one of his generals the task of conquering the Ionians. [154] But as soon as Cyrus had left Sardis, Pactyes incited the Lydians to revolt from Tabalus and Cyrus, and, as he controlled all the gold from Sardis, he went down to the sea and hired mercenaries and persuaded the men of the coast to join his army. He then marched to Sardis, where he besieged Tabalus, who was shut up in the citadel.

Herodotus 1.153.3-154

Cyrus installed the Persian Tabalus as governor of Sardis, acting on his behalf while he continued his military campaigns. Leaving a Lydian in control of the financial administration of Sardis proved to be a mistake, which Cyrus immediately rectified by appointing the Mede Harpagus in his stead. Tabalus is the first known Persian satrap appointed to office in the Persian empire (see **123-127**).

Herodotus is well informed about Cyrus' strategy of conquest, perhaps from oral accounts he heard in Asia Minor. According to the Babylonian Nabonidus Chronicle, Cyrus' conquest began with Media, followed by Lydia and Babylon. No Near Eastern source reports on the eastern campaigns of Cyrus, but it is more than likely that Cyrus' army marched east after the conquest of Babylon in 539/8. Ctesias dates the defeat of Bactria and the Scythians before Cyrus' campaign against Lydia (*FGrH* 688 F9.10), but Cyrus may have regarded the subjection of the 'old empires' - with the exception of Egypt - as strategically more important to form a base of power, before setting off with his troops for the east. Evidence for Cyrus' conquest of Bactria is indirectly provided by the Inscription of Bisitun (DB III: §38, **44**) which mentions the satrap Dadaršiš who was in office there in 522. The Scythians, or Saka, were nomadic tribes who came from the regions of the Ukraine and Central Asia. Bordering on the northern part of the Persian empire, some of the

Scythian tribes, the Amyrgian Scythians, the Scythians with pointed caps, and the Scythians from Across-the-Sea (Black Sea), had become subjects of the Persian empire under Cyrus (see below DSe, **46**). In 517 Darius I led an unsuccessful campaign against the Scythians (Hdt 4.83.1). Cyrus died in 530 while on campaign against the Massagetae, a people who lived in the region between the eastern shore of the Caspian Sea and the Aral Sea. He had ruled for twenty-nine years (Hdt.1.214). His son and successor Cambyses II carried out his father's plans to conquer Egypt (see below **19-24**).

The tomb of Cyrus

17   [3.6] He (*Alexander III, the Great*) went to Pasargadae; this, too, was an ancient royal residence. In it he saw the tomb of Cyrus, situated in a *paradeisos*; the tower-like building was not large, and was concealed within the trees. The tomb had a solid base, but had a roof and a burial-chamber above it. The latter had a very narrow entrance.

Strabo 15.3.6

After Alexander the Great had conquered Persia, he visited the tomb of Cyrus II to pay his respects to the founder of the empire. The tomb, a rectangular structure with only one chamber and a gabled roof, stands on a platform constructed of six huge steps. It is located near the Audience Hall and the Royal Residence of Cyrus, and can still be seen today. At the time of the Persian empire, the tomb stood within a *paradeisos*, a royal garden (see below **110-111**).

1.4. CAMBYSES II

First Babylonian document dated to the reign of Cambyses

18   An eight-year-old red ass which is not branded, belonging to Nidinti-Bel, son of Bunene-ibni; he sold (it) for fifty shekels of silver, for the full price, to Bel-ušal-lim, son of Gimullu, of the family Eppeš-ili. Nidinti-Bel, son of Bunene-ibni, bears responsibility for the *uškutu* of the ass.
  Witnesses: Nabu-šum-ukin son of Nergal-ušallim of the family Šigu'a, Ina-teši-etir son of Ina-Esagil-[...] of the family of Balihu.
  Scribe: Rimut-Bel son of Bel-iqiša of the family Bel-etir.
  Babylon, 12 Ululu, accession year of Cambyses, king of Babylon, king of lands.

Strassmeier 1890: no.1 (transl. H. Baker)

The tablet text records the sale of an ass for fifty shekels in the city of Babylon. Nidinti-Bel perhaps has to stand surety for the ass. Documents were customarily dated by the regnal year of the king. The date is always stated at the end of the document, after listing the witnesses of the exchange, the name of the scribe, as well as the place of the sale. The date given in this text, the twelfth day of the month Ululu, is 31 August 530, and provides the earliest reference for the reign of Cambyses II. His title is given in accordance with the Babylonian royal title as 'king of Babylon, king of lands'.

Documents from Egypt

Hieroglyphic seal inscription of Cambyses

19   The King of Upper and Lower Egypt, Cambyses, beloved of (the goddess) Wadjet, ruler (of the city) of Imet, the great one, Eye of the Sun, ruler of the sky, mistress of the gods, given life like (that of) Re (the sun god).

Hodjache, Berlev 1977: 37–9

The inscription documents Cambyses' role as the king of Egypt, which he conquered in 525. By using a seal with a hieroglyphic script, and by claiming to enjoy the favour of the Egyptian goddess Wadjet, Cambyses presented himself as a foreign ruler respecting Egyptian custom and religion. Wadjet was the Egyptian goddess of the city of Imet. She protected the king and also symbolised the unity between Upper and Lower Egypt, the traditional division of Egypt between the Valley of the Nile (Upper Egypt) and the Nile Delta (Lower Egypt). The city of Imet, modern Tell Nabasha, is situated near Husseiniya in the eastern Delta. Herodotus knew the city under the name Buto (Hdt.2.75.1). (For a different city bearing the same name, but located in the western Delta, see **28**)

Hieroglyphic inscription of Udjahorresnet

20 (...) The one honoured by Neith the Great One, the mother of the god, and by the gods of Saïs, the prince, count, royal seal-bearer, sole companion, true king's acquaintance, his beloved, the scribe, inspector in the assembly, overseer of scribes, great leader, administrator of the palace, commander of the king's navy under the King of Upper and Lower Egypt Ankhkare (*Psammetichus III*), Udjahorresnet; engendered by the administrator of the castles (of the red crown), chief-of-Pe priest, *rnp*-priest, he who embraces the Eye of Horus, priest of Neith who presides over the Nome of Saïs, Peftuaneith. He says: 'The Great King of all foreign lands, Cambyses, came to Egypt, and the foreigners of all foreign lands were with him. He rules the entire land. They made their dwellings therein, and he was the Great King of Egypt, the Great King of all foreign lands. His Majesty assigned to me the office of chief physician. He caused me to be beside him as a companion administrator of the palace. I made his royal titulary, his name being the King of Upper Egypt and Lower Egypt Mesuti-Re (*Cambyses*).

'I caused His Majesty to perceive the greatness of Saïs, that it is the seat of Neith the Great, the mother who bore Re, who began birth when no birth had yet been; and the nature of the greatness of the temple of Neith: that it is heaven in every aspect; and the nature of the greatness of the temples of Neith and also of all the gods and goddesses who are in them; and the nature of the greatness of the Temple of the King, that it is the seat of the Sovereign, the Lord of Heaven (*Osiris*); and the nature of the greatness of the Resenet and Mehenet sanctuaries; and of the House of Re and the House of Atum; that is, the mystery of all gods (...).

'I petitioned the Majesty of the King of Upper and Lower Egypt, Cambyses, about all the foreigners who were dwelling in the temple of Neith, so that they should be expelled from it in order to let the temple of Neith be in all its splendour, as it had been in existence since the beginning. His Majesty commanded to expel all the foreigners who dwelt in the temple of Neith; all their houses were demolished and their pollution that was in this temple. They carried [all their] personal belongings outside the wall of the temple. His Majesty commanded to purify the temple of Neith and to return all its personnel, the [...] and the hour-priests of the temple. His Majesty commanded that offerings should be given to Neith the Great, the mother of the god, and to the great gods who are in Saïs, as it was before. His Majesty commanded (to perform) all their festivals and all their processions, as had been done since antiquity. His Majesty did this because I had caused His Majesty to perceive the greatness of Saïs, that it is the city of all the gods, who remain on their thrones in it forever.'

The one honoured by the gods of Saïs, the chief physician, Udjahorresnet, says: 'The King of Upper and Lower Egypt, Cambyses, came to Saïs. His Majesty proceeded himself to the temple of Neith. He touched the ground with his forehead before Her Majesty very greatly as every king has done. He made a great offering of all good things to Neith the Great, the mother of the god, and the great gods who are in Saïs, as every excellent king has done. His Majesty did this because I had caused His Majesty to perceive the greatness of Her Majesty, for she is the mother of Re himself.' (...)

Posener 1936:1–26; Lichtheim 1960: 36–41

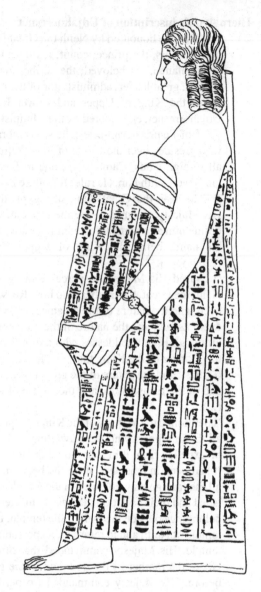

2. Statue of Udjahorresnet

The text is inscribed on the statue of Udjahorresnet, which was probably erected in the temple of Osiris at Saïs, modern Sa al-Hagar, in the northwest of the Nile Delta. The statue is now in the Vatican Museum in Rome (Vatican Collections no.196; the head is not original). In this text Udjahorresnet records his career under Cambyses II and Darius I, providing an example of an Egyptian official working under Persian rule.

Udjahorresnet had already served as a naval commander under the pharaohs Amasis (570-526) and Psammetichus (526-525), before he became the 'chief physician' under Cambyses II. Cambyses is referred to by the Egyptian royal title of 'King of Upper and Lower Egypt', as well as by a personal royal name, Mesuti-Re, 'Offspring of Re'. Re, or Ra, is the Egyptian sun and the sun god himself. Following the Egyptian tradition of kingship, the Persian kings as pharaohs were given a semi-divine status in Egypt. Udjahorresnet takes credit for drawing Cambyses' attention to the need for restoration of the temple of the goddess Neith at Saïs, which had been the seat and capital of the previous Egyptian dynasty. Neith, the Egyptian goddess who appeared in human form crowned with the red crown of Lower Egypt, was especially honoured by the Egyptian kings because they stood under her particular protection (see Hdt.2.175 for Amasis' building work at her temple and Hdt.3.16.1 for Cambyses' visit to Saïs).

Cambyses pursued the same policy of political and religious integration as his father Cyrus II. He honoured the country's gods, restored the temples, ensured that the religious rituals were carried out, and in his respect for the religious tradition followed his Egyptian predecessors. To all appearance, Cambyses wanted to be regarded as the just king under whose (foreign) reign life continues exactly as it had done under the country's own good kings. Udjahorresnet's case also demonstrates that the local élite was not excluded from the royal court life and could prosper under the Persian kings.

Epitaph for the Apis bull interred in the Serapeum in Memphis in 524

21   [Year] 6, third month of the season of Shemu, day 10(?) (*November 524*), under the Majesty of the King of Upper and Lower Egypt, Mesuti-Re, given life forever. The god was taken up [in peace towards the perfect West and was laid to rest in his place in the necropolis], in the place which His Majesty has made for him, [after] all [the ceremonies had been performed for him] in the Hall of Embalming. Sets of linen were made for him [...], there were brought [to him his amulets and all his ornaments in gold] and in all precious materials [...] temple of Ptah, which is within Hemag [...] ordered [...] towards Memphis, saying: 'You may lead [...].' All was done that His Majesty had ordered [...] in year 27 [...] (of Apis) in year [...] of Cambyses [...]

Posener 1936: no. 3

Inscription on the sarcophagus of the Apis bull

22   Horus, the Uniter of the Two Lands, the King of Upper and Lower Egypt, Mesuti-Re, son of Re, Cambyses, may he live forever: He made as his memorial for his father, Apis-Osiris, a great sarcophagus of granite, dedicated by the King of Upper and Lower Egypt, Mesuti-Re, son of Re, Cambyses, given all life, duration, and power, all health, all joy, appearing as King of Upper and Lower Egypt, forever.

Posener 1936: no.4

The epitaph on the stele in ill. 3 (**21**) and the inscription on the sarcophagus (**22**), both now in the Louvre Museum in Paris, testify to the fact that Cambyses honoured the death of the sacred Apis bull with proper funerary rites. The god Ptah, principal god of Memphis, the ancient capital of Egypt, uttered oracles through the Apis bull. Ptah was the god of skilled workers and artisans, the creator of the world, of the heart, and of speech. The Apis bull was selected according to specific marks on its forehead, neck and flanks, before its official enthronement, and played a role in the royal rituals at Memphis. After its death the Apis bull was renamed Apis-Osiris, and was buried in the necropolis of the Apis bulls, the Serapeum. Horus is the Egyptian god of the world and of the light, represented as a child or as a falcon; the name Hemag is an epithet for the god Osiris, but in the above text implies a space within the temple.

In the epitaph, which was set up in November 524, Cambyses acknowledges Apis as his divine father, while the inscription on the sarcophagus clearly identifies him as the recognised king of Egypt. The inscriptions dispose of the notion expressed in Herodotus (see **23**) that the burial was kept secret from Cambyses. Most importantly, it disproves the accusation that Cambyses showed no respect for the cult of the Apis bull and that he had murdered the animal. The bull had died a natural death about one year after Cambyses' conquest of Egypt. Cambyses pursued his father's policy of publicly respecting local cults and religions. The new Apis bull was born in May 525 and died in the fourth year of the reign of Darius I (518/7) (for his epitaph see below **51**).

Greek evidence on the killing of the Apis bull

23   [27.1] After Cambyses had reached Memphis, the Apis bull, that the Greeks call Epaphus, appeared to the Egyptians. On its appearance, the Egyptians put on their

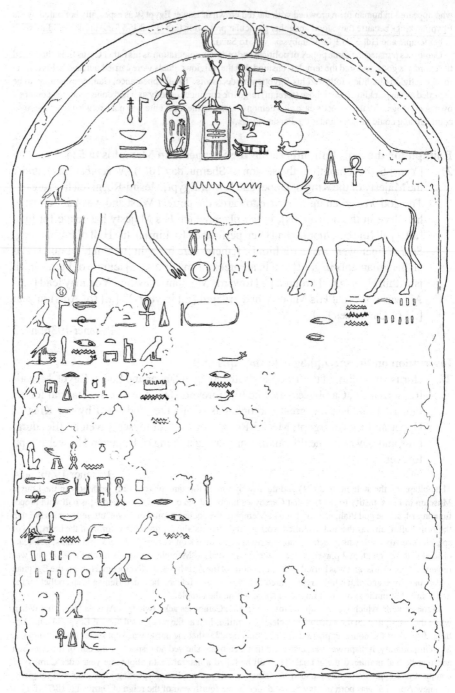

3. Cambyses' stele for the Apis bull

best clothes and celebrated a festival. [27.2] When Cambyses saw the Egyptians acting in this manner, he was convinced that they were rejoicing over his recent reverses (**26**); so he summoned the rulers of Memphis (...). [27.3] They told him that a god who revealed himself from time to time had now appeared to them and that all Egypt rejoiced and celebrated a feast whenever he did so. Hearing this, Cambyses replied that they were lying and he had them executed as liars.

[28.1] Having put them to death, he then summoned the priests before him. When they gave him the same answer, he said that if a tame god had come to the Egyptians, he would know it, and saying no more, he bade the priests bring the Apis bull. So they went and brought the Apis bull. [28.2] This Apis, or Epaphus, is a calf born of a cow that can never conceive again. According to the Egyptians, the cow is made pregnant by a light from heaven, and thereafter gives birth to Apis. [28.3] The marks of this calf called Apis are these: it is black, with a three-cornered white spot on its forehead, and one resembling an eagle on its back; the hairs under the tail are double, and there is a knot under the tongue.

[29.1] When the priests returned, bringing Apis with them, Cambyses, who was half mad, drew his dagger and aimed at the belly of the animal, but instead stabbed it in the thigh; laughing, he said to the priests: [29.2] 'You numskulls, are these your gods, animals of flesh and blood which can feel an iron weapon? A god worthy of the Egyptians indeed. But you shall pay dearly for having made me a laughing-stock.' When he had said this, he ordered those whose duty it was to flog the priests, and if they found any other Egyptian celebrating the festival, to kill him. [29.3] Thus the festival ended and the priests were punished; Apis lay in the temple, wounded in the thigh. When it died of its wound, the priests buried it without Cambyses knowing about it.

[30.1] According to the Egyptians, Cambyses, who even before had not been in his right mind, now went mad because of this crime.

Herodotus 3.27–30.1

The story of Cambyses' killing of the Apis bull is part of the negative propaganda against the Persian king, which must originate in Egypt. This sacrilege is one of three atrocities Cambyses is accused of: the killing of his brother Bardiya, called Smerdis in Herodotus, the murder of his pregnant sister-wife, and the killing of the Apis bull. Cambyses' alleged lack of respect for the religious cults of Egypt and his sacrilegious killing of the Apis bull stand in sharp contrast to Cyrus' public acknowledgement and support of foreign cults; this serves to portray Cambyses' character as one contrasting with the noble and humble character of Cyrus, as well as depicting him as a mad ruler. Herodotus' language is quite explicit concerning Cambyses (Gr. *hypomargoteros*), leaving no doubt about his insanity. The particular spice in the story about the killing of the Apis bull is the manner of its death: in an ironic twist of fate Cambyses dies in exactly the same manner, by stabbing himself in the thigh (see below **27-29**). For Cambyses' respect for foreign cults see below **24, 205**.

Demotic document from Egypt on financial administration under Cambyses

24 [1] Those matters which shall be discussed in the Court of Law concerning the rights of the temples. [2] Building-wood, fire-wood, linen and shrubs(?), which before were given to the temples of the gods, [3] at the time of the Pharaoh Amasis, with the exception of the temple of Memphis, the temple of Wenkhem, and the temple of Perapis (...)(?), [4] regarding these temples, Cambyses ordered thus: 'It may not be allowed to give these to them [...]! May they be given [5] a space in the marshes and in the southern land (*Upper Egypt*), so that they provide building-wood and fire-wood for themselves, [6] and offer it to their gods.'

Concerning the tribute to the above mentioned three temples, Cambyses ordered thus: 'May it (*the tribute*) be returned to them, [7] as it was previously.' The cattle which have been given to the temples of the gods before, [8] at the time of the Pharaoh Amasis, except for the above mentioned three temples, concerning it Cambyses ordered thus: [9] 'Their share is what is given to them. What was given to the above mentioned three temples, they were ordered to return it (to them).' [10] In regard to the fowl which formerly, in the time of Pharaoh Amasis had been given to the temples, [11] except for the three temples, Cambyses ordered thus: 'Do not give it to them! The priests should raise geese (themselves) [12] and offer them to the gods.' In regard to the amount of the silver, the cattle, the fowl, the grain (and) the other things [13] which were in the past, in the time of the Pharaoh Amasis, given to the temples, Cambyses had ordered: [14] 'Do not give it to the gods!'

The total of the listed goods amounts to:160,532 pieces(?), [...], grain [15] 170,210, (bread?) 6,000, Total: 376,400 [...](?)[...][16] frankincense, fire-wood, shrubs?, papyrus, building-wood - a copy of this list (is in) another papyrus roll. [17] Building-wood: a copy of this matter (is listed in)[...]

BN 215, Spiegelberg 1914, Devauchelle 1995

The Demotic Chronicle was written on the *verso*, the reverse page, of a papyrus document. Demotic is an ancient Egyptian popular form of writing. The provenance of the text is not known, but one possibility is that it came from Memphis. It is now in the Bibliothèque Nationale in Paris. The Demotic text probably dates to the second half of the third century BC.

The text offers a glimpse of Cambyses' financial policy in Egypt. Though the papyrus is partly broken and the text partly illegible, it can be established that Cambyses pursued a harsh policy towards the Egyptian temples, except for the temple of Ptah at Memphis, the temple of Wenkhem, north of Memphis, and the Heliopolitan temple of the Nile, Pi-ha'p-en-Ôn, which perhaps stood on the site of Egyptian Babylon. The temple economy of Egypt was able to amass considerable wealth, and it may be that through some incident unknown to us Cambyses felt compelled to curtail the temples' power. One possibility is that this policy was imposed in consequence of a revolt in Egypt, which may have taken place in 524/3, but which is not recorded in the surviving sources. Cambyses had followed his father's policy of 'religious tolerance' in Egypt, aiming at the continuity of religious and cultural life; yet the papyrus clearly attests a change in this policy for all temples except the three mentioned in the text. It is possible that Herodotus' Egyptian informants were descendants of those priests whose privileged position had been curtailed by Cambyses' policy. This would certainly explain the emphasis on Cambyses' alleged sacrileges mentioned by Herodotus. It is also the case that the three atrocious deeds of Cambyses recorded by Herodotus are all connected with Cambyses' stay in Egypt (see Hdt.3.29-31, **32**).

The African expeditions of Cambyses

25   [17.1] After this (*the events in Egypt*) Cambyses wanted to undertake three campaigns, against the Carchedonians (*Carthaginians*), against the Ammonians and against the long-lived Ethiopians (*Nubians*) who live in Libya on the borders of the southern sea. (...) [17.2] Taking advice, he decided to send a naval force against the Carchedonians, and part of the infantry against the Ammonians; to Ethiopia he first would send out spies (...).

Herodotus 3.17

26   [25.4] But before his army had accomplished a fifth part of the march (*into Ethiopia*), they had consumed all their provisions, and after the food was eaten, they ate the beasts of burden until they also had all been eaten. (...) [25.7] When he learned about this, Cambyses, aghast at the cannibalism, abandoned his expedition against Ethiopia and led his army back again. (...). [26.1] As for those who were sent against the Ammonians, they marched out, setting off from Thebes with guides; it is known that they reached the town of Oasis (*el-Khargeh*; see below **195-196**)(...). [26.2] It is said that this is as far as the army went; except for the Ammonians themselves and those who heard from them, nobody can say anything further about them, for neither did they reach the Ammonians nor did they return. [26.3] This is what the Ammonians themselves say: when they (*the Persians*) were marching across the desert from Oasis to attack them and were about halfway between Oasis and their country, an exceptionally violent south wind blew up as they were eating their mid-day meal and buried them in the masses of sand which it bore, and so they disappeared.

Herodotus 3.25.4–26.3

Cambyses' three expeditions into African territory may have been planned to secure the western and southern regions of Egypt. Herodotus describes the expeditions as disastrous military failures, and these exaggerated accounts serve to underline the insanity of Cambyses. No Near Eastern source corroborates these accounts. However, Herodotus concedes that Cambyses secured at least part of Ethiopia (Nubia) for the Persian empire during this campaign, and remarks that the Ethiopians were among those peoples belonging to the Persian empire who brought gifts to the king (Hdt.3.97.2). Cambyses took control of at least part of Nubia beyond the First Cataract, located near the 24th degree of latitude, including the island of Elephantine. Here, a Jewish military colony was stationed and from then on served under the Persian kings (see below **205**). According to Strabo (17.1.5), Cambyses even reached the Third Cataract, taking control of the city of Meroe.

The death of Cambyses

27   In the month Garmapada nine days had passed (*1 July 522*), and then he (*Bardiya/Gaumata*) seized the kingship. Afterwards Cambyses died his own death.

35§11

'Died his own death' should mean that Cambyses died of natural causes, rather than 'died by his own hand', which could mean either by suicide or through his own fault. This laconic remark made in the Bisitun Inscription about Cambyses' death fails to shed any light on the circumstances in which Cambyses died or on his possible reaction to Gaumata's uprising. Cambyses died some time after 1 July 522 (see the reference to Cambyses' death in the Demotic papyrus from Egypt, **55**). (For full discussion of the Bisitun Inscription see below **44**.)

28   [64.3] As he (*Cambyses*) was springing onto his horse, the cap slipped off the scabbard of his sword, and the naked blade struck his thigh, wounding him in the same part where he himself had once struck the Egyptian god Apis. Believing the blow to be mortal, Cambyses asked what was the name of the town where he was. They told him it was Ecbatana. [64.4] He had already had a prophecy from Buto, that he would end his life in Ecbatana. Cambyses had thought this meant that he would die in old age in Median Ecbatana, his capital city, but as events proved, the oracle prophesied his death in Ecbatana in Syria (*near Mount Carmel*).

Herodotus 3.64.3–4

Herodotus describes Cambyses' death as an ironic twist of fate. Not only does he die in exactly the same manner as that in which he had allegedly killed the Apis bull (see **23**)—perhaps signifying 'just punishment' for his sacrilege—but he also misunderstood the prophecy in his identification of Ecbatana.

29   When he (*Cambyses*) arrived in Babylon, he cut a piece of wood with his cutlass, by way of passing the time, and he cuts himself in the thigh right into the muscle and dies eleven days later, after a reign of eighteen years. (...) Izabates took Cambyses' body and brought it back to Parsa (*Persepolis*).

Ctesias *FGrH* 688 F 13

Ctesias' mentioning of Parsa is understood to refer to Persepolis itself. Archaeological evidence suggests that the tomb of Cambyses was built near Persepolis, and that the location of Persepolis had already been selected by Cambyses as the site of a new royal city. It was left to Darius I to carry out his plans.

1.5. BARDIYA

Bardiya, full brother of Cambyses

30   Cambyses had a brother, Bardiya by name, of the same mother and the same
father as Cambyses. Afterwards Cambyses killed Bardiya. When Cambyses had
killed Bardiya, it did not become known to the people that Bardiya had been
killed. Afterwards Cambyses went to Egypt. When Cambyses had set out for
Egypt, the people became disloyal. The Lie grew greatly in the land, in Persia,
Media, and the other countries.

DB I: §10

Darius' only reference in the Bisitun Inscription to the reign of his predecessor is negative, accusing
Cambyses of having killed his brother Bardiya. Darius stresses that they were full brothers. The Persian king
could have several wives (see below **176-180**). According to Darius' version of events, the murder took
place before Cambyses set out for Egypt in 527, though it was not common knowledge. Only then did a
revolt break out back in Persia (**32**).

The expression 'the Lie grew greatly in the land' means that the values supported by the god Ahura Mazda
had been overturned in favour of upheaval and revolt.

31   Fourth in succession, Cyrus' son ruled the land.
Fifth Mardus, who disgraced his realm and ancient throne;
But the brave Artaphrenes with his friends conspired
and killed him in his palace.

Aeschylus, Persians 774-777

In Aeschylus' *Persians*, performed in 472, Bardiya's name is given as Mardus. Aeschylus has a different
perception of Bardiya as a ruler who damaged the Persian monarchy. He erroneously names Artaphrenes as
the Persian who killed Bardiya.

32   [30.1] His (*Cambyses'*) first evil act was the slaying of his brother Smerdis, who
had the same father and mother. He had already sent him back to Persia out of
envy, because he alone amongst the Persians could draw the bow which the Fish-
eaters had brought from Ethiopia, a distance of two fingers' breadth; no other
Persian could draw it at all. [30.2] When Smerdis had gone to Persia, Cambyses
dreamt that a messenger came from Persia and told him that Smerdis was sitting
on the royal throne with his head reaching heaven. [30.3] Therefore, fearing that
his brother would kill him and rule in his stead, he sent Prexaspes, the most loyal
of the Persians, to Persia to kill him. He went up to Susa and killed Smerdis; some
say he went out hunting with him, others, that he took him to the Erythraean Sea
(*Persian Gulf*) and drowned him there.

Herodotus 3.30

In Herodotus' story Cambyses, already in Egypt, ordered his brother Bardiya, called Smerdis in Herodotus,
to leave Egypt and return to Persia. The reason Herodotus gives for his doing so seems unlikely. Suspecting
Bardiya of wanting to take over his kingship, Cambyses entrusted Prexaspes, father of Aspathines, with his
murder. It is possible that Cambyses had appointed his brother Bardiya as regent in Persis, while he himself
was away on campaign.

33   [7.11] 'To you, Tanaoxares, I give the satrapies of Media, Armenia and in addition to those two Cadusia. And in giving you this position, I consider that I leave
to your older brother greater power and the title of king, while to you I leave a
happiness disturbed by fewer cares.'

Xenophon, Cyropaedia 8.7.11

According to Xenophon, Bardiya, called Tanaoxares in the *Cyropaedia*, was Cambyses' younger brother,
whom his father Cyrus appointed as satrap. Xenophon and Ctesias differ over which satrapies were under
his control (see **34**).

34 When Cyrus was about to die, he appointed his first son Cambyses great king, and his younger son Tanyoxarkes as ruler of the Bactrians and their lands, as well as the Chorasmians, the Parthians and the Carmanians, emphasising that he should have these lands without their tribute.

Ctesias FGrH 688 F 9.8

Bardiya, here named as Tanyoxarkes, is mentioned as the younger brother of Cambyses, who was appointed satrap of Bactria and other eastern provinces.

Gaumata, calling himself Bardiya

35 §11. Darius the king says: 'Afterwards there was one man, a *magus*, Gaumata by name. He rose up from Paishiyauvada - from a mountain called Arakadri. In the month Viyaxna (Bab. *Addaru*) fourteen days had passed when he rose up (*11 March 522*). He lied to the people thus: "I am Bardiya the son of Cyrus, the brother of Cambyses." Afterwards all the people rebelled against Cambyses and went over to him, both Persia and Media, and the other countries. He seized the kingship. In the month Garmapada (Bab. *Du'zu*) nine days had passed (*1 July 522*), and then he seized the kingship. Afterwards Cambyses died his own death.'
§12. Darius the king says: 'The kingship, which Gaumata the *magus* had seized from Cambyses, had from ancient times belonged to our family. Then Gaumata the *magus* took from Cambyses both Persia and Media and the other countries. He took (them) and made them his own property. He became king.'
§13. Darius the king says: 'There was no man, neither a Persian nor a Mede nor anyone of our family, who might have taken the kingship from that Gaumata the *magus*. The people feared him greatly, since he used to slay in great number the people who previously had known Bardiya. For this reason he used to slay the people: "That they may not know me, that I am not Bardiya, the son of Cyrus." No one dared say anything about Gaumata the *magus* until I came. Afterwards I prayed to Ahura Mazda. Ahura Mazda brought me aid. In the month Bagayadiš (Bab. *Tašritu*) ten days had passed (*29 September 522*), then I with a few men slew Gaumata the *magus* and the men who were his foremost followers. A fortress Sikayuvatiš by name and a district Nisaya by name, in Media - there I slew him. I took the kingship from him. By the favour of Ahura Mazda I became king. Ahura Mazda bestowed the kingship upon me.'
§ 14. Darius the king says: 'I restored the kingship which had been taken away from our family, that I restored. I re-installed it in its proper place. Just as they had been previously, so I restored the sanctuaries which Gaumata the *magus* had destroyed. I restored to the people the farmsteads, the livestock, the servants and the houses which Gaumata the *magus* had taken away from them. I re-installed the people in their proper places. I restored Persia, Media and the other lands what had been taken away, just as they were previously. By the favour of Ahura Mazda I did this. I strove until I had restored our royal house to its proper place, as it was previously. So I strove by the favour of Ahura Mazda, so that Gaumata the *magus* did not take away our royal house.'
§15. Darius the king says: 'This (is) what I have done after becoming king.'

DB I: §11–15

The Bisitun Inscription is our primary account of the events relating to the revolt of Gaumata, who claimed to be Bardiya, the brother of Cambyses. The Bisitun Inscription relates these events from the perspective of Darius I, who succeeded to the throne after the death of Gaumata. Darius' presentation of these events for his contemporaries and for posterity to see and understand may be a skilful piece of propaganda to justify his accession to the throne and to legitimise his kingship. For full text and comment on the Bisitun Inscription see **44**.

On 11 March 522 a *magus* (see below **192–194**) called Gaumata rebelled against Cambyses, claiming to be Bardiya. The location of the place of his uprising, Paishiyauvada, has not yet been identified. The core lands, Persia and Media, as well as other countries, rebelled against Cambyses. By 1 July 522 Gaumata was recognised as king. Darius accuses Gaumata of leading a regime of terror, killing those who knew the real Bardiya.

Gaumata's unlawful rule came to an end on 29 September, when Darius killed him in a fortress called Sikayuvatiš in Media. This fortress was probably located somewhere near Mount Bisitun, where Darius carved his inscription to commemorate this decisive event, which effectively made him king of Persia (see below **44**). He attributed his victory to the Persian god Ahura Mazda, under whose protection he fought.

Darius presents Gaumata, the false Bardiya, as usurper, whose reign was marked by terror. He is said to have destroyed sanctuaries and confiscated people's property and livestock. Exactly which group of people Darius is referring to is difficult to decide. It is unlikely that Gaumata confiscated the property of the Persian nobility, because he would have alienated them and created a significant opposition. He may have taken steps to ensure that all, or a part, of the Persian nobility remained loyal to him.

Darius' picture of Gaumata contrasts sharply with the version given by Herodotus, according to which Gaumata was favoured by the people because he offered three years without military service and exemption from tribute payments for all the countries of the empire (see below **36–40**).

The difficult question is to decide whether Darius' version is historical truth or merely political propaganda meant to help secure the Persian throne for himself. Opinions are divided between the view that a *magus* called Gaumata did revolt against Persia, and the view that Gaumata did not exist, and that it was in fact the 'real' Bardiya who was killed by Darius I.

The 'usurper' Bardiya

36 [61.1] While Cambyses son of Cyrus was spending time in Egypt and was half-mad, two *magi* who were brothers revolted against him, one of whom Cambyses had left as steward of his household. He now began the revolt, being aware that the death of Smerdis had been kept secret and that only a few of the Persians knew about it, while most of them believed that he was still alive. [61.2] Therefore he planned to seize the kingship. The brother whom I have mentioned as participating in the plot strongly resembled Smerdis son of Cyrus, the brother of Cambyses, who had killed him; he not only bore resemblance to Smerdis, but he also had the same name, Smerdis. [61.3] The other *magus* Patizeithes, who had convinced him that he would carry out the plot, took him and sat him on the royal throne. Having done so, he sent heralds out to Egypt and elsewhere to announce to the army that they had henceforth to obey Smerdis son of Cyrus, and not Cambyses.

Herodotus 3.61

Herodotus' story of the 'false Smerdis' is a more elaborate version of Darius' story of Gaumata pretending to be Bardiya. In this version, two *magi* plan to overthrow the Persian throne, one of whom bears a striking resemblance to the true Smerdis/Bardiya. This unlikely resemblance becomes central for the development of Herodotus' story, since the unmasking of the 'false Smerdis' is due only to a cunning action on the part of Otanes and his daughter Phaidyme (**177**).

37 [67.2] After the death of Cambyses, the *magus* reigned in security, pretending to be Smerdis, son of Cyrus, for the seven months needed to complete Cambyses' eight-year rule. [67.3] In this time he greatly benefited his subjects, so much so that after his death all the people of Asia, except the Persians, wanted him back. For the *magus* proclaimed to all peoples three years' freedom from military service and paying tribute.

Herodotus 3.67.2–3

Herodotus depicts Bardiya/Smerdis as a benign ruler, who won the people's support through tax exemption and relief from military service. Such measures would have ensured his support among the people, and would explain the rebellions against Darius I after his restoration of the laws (**35** §14).

38 [70.1] Otanes took aside Aspathines and Gobryas, leading Persians whom he regarded as most trustworthy, and related everything to them. They themselves had suspected that this (*the magus' posing as Bardiya*) was the case and believed what Otanes told them. [70.2] They decided that each of them should take as an accomplice the Persian whom he most trusted. Otanes chose Intaphernes, Gobryas Megabyxus, and Aspathines Hydarnes. [70.3] They were now six in number when Darius son of Hystaspes arrived at Susa from Persia, where his father was *hyparchos*. On his arrival the six Persians decided to make him an accomplice.

Herodotus 3.70

See **44**: §68. For Aspathines and Gobryas see **112-115**.

39 [78.4] Two of the seven, Darius and Gobryas, burst into the room with him (*the magus*). Gobryas grappled with the *magus*, while Darius stood over them, not knowing what to do, because it was dark and he was afraid of striking Gobryas. [78.5] Realising that he was standing idly by, Gobryas asked him why his hand was idle; 'I am afraid of striking you', he answered. But Gobryas said: 'Strike through us both, if need be.' Darius did as he said, and by good fortune struck the *magus* with his dagger.

Herodotus 3.78.4–5

40 [11] A *magus* called Sphendadates, who had committed a crime and had been whipped by Tanyoxarkes, went to Cambyses and slandered his (*Cambyses'*) brother Tanyoxarkes, claiming that he was plotting against him. To prove the disloyalty of Tanyoxarkes, he claimed that if he (*Cambyses*) would summon him to come to him, he would not come. Thus Cambyses orders his brother to come to him, but because other matters forced him to stay, he put off coming. The *magus* now brings more accusations against him. But Amytis, his mother, who suspected the bad intentions of the *magus*, advised her son Cambyses not to believe him; Cambyses replied that he did not believe him, but in fact believed him completely. [12] When Cambyses ordered his brother to come the third time he came. His brother (*Cambyses*) embraces him without abandoning his plan to kill him, and without the knowledge of Amytis he hurried to turn his intentions into action.

The *magus*, sharing the king's counsel, advises the following plan: he, the *magus*, strongly resembled Tanyoxarkes; therefore he advises Cambyses to make a public declaration that he has to cut off his head for making false accusations against Tanyoxarkes, and to kill Tanyoxarkes in secret and dress the *magus* up in his clothes, so that by his clothing too he would be thought to be Tanyoxarkes. So it is done. Tanyoxarkes is killed by bull's blood which he drank. The *magus* puts on his clothes and is thought to be Tanyoxarkes. [13] For a long time he deceives everybody, except for Artasyras, Bagapates and Izabates, the only people Cambyses had informed about the plan. (...) He is sent to Bactria and he acts just like Tanyoxarkes. After five years have passed, Amytis is informed about the tragedy by the eunuch Tibetheus, whom the *magus* had hit. She asks for Sphendadates from Cambyses. He does not give him to her. She curses him, drinks poison and dies.

Ctesias *FGrH* 688 F 13.11–13

The *magus*, here called Sphendadates, is described as having intrigued against Cambyses' brother because of a personal grudge. Ctesias gives a completely different chronology of events, allowing the *magus* to act as Tanyoxarkes for several years, living in Bactria (as satrap?). Only after the death of Cambyses does the *magus* become king. The idea of a revolt by Cambyses' brother or his impersonator, is completely omitted in this version. According to Herodotus (**176**), Cassandane was the mother of Cambyses.

Babylonian documents dating Bardiya's acceptance in Babylon

41   [x+]1/2 mina of white silver belonging to Nabu-šum-usur, son of Šapik-zeri of the family of Misiraya, the debt of Nabu-šum-usur, son of Mušezib-Marduk of the family of Šumu-libši; each mina will accrue one shekel of silver per month (as interest); from the first day of Simannu (*the 3rd month*) he will pay interest; each month he will pay interest.

Witnesses: Nadin, son of Balatu, of the family of Šumu-libši; Marduk-šum-iddin, son of Bel-nadin-apli, of the family of Šumu-libši; Muranu, son of Nabu-dannu-ilani, of the family Misiraya; Guzanu, son of Nabu-na'id; Le'ea.

Scribe: Nabu-ahhe-iddin son of Nabu-šum-lišir, of the family of Saggilaya.

Babylon, Ayyaru, accession year of Barziya, king of Babylon, king of lands.

Strassmeier 1889: no.1 (transl. H. Baker)

42   Eleven and a half minas of white silver, of one-eighth alloy, the debt of Nabu-ban-apli, with the promissory note for three minas and ten shekels of silver drawn up in the month Tebetu, and the promissory note for three and a half minas of silver drawn up in the month Addaru, Marduk-šum-usur son of Aplaya of the family Bel-eteru is owed by Itti-Marduk-balatu son of Nabu-ahhe-iddin of the family Egibi; from the first day of the month Ayyaru the said silver, 11 1/2 minas, will accrue 1 shekel per mina per month (as interest). Excluding two previous promissory notes for 14 minas of silver.

Witnesses: Itti-Nabu-balatu son of Zubbatu-ilu, Nabu-mukin-zeri son of Nabu-šar-usur, Nabu-ban-ahi, courtier.

Scribe: Nabu-šum-iddin son of Šulaya of the family Ea-eppeš-ili.

Humadešu, day 19 (of the month) Nisannu, year 1 of Barziya, king of lands.

Strassmeier 1889: no.2 (transl. H. Baker)

The first text records the interest payment imposed on the debt of Nabu-šum-usur the son of Mušezib-Marduk. For each mina he owes to Nabu-šum-usur the son of Šapik-zeri, he has to pay one shekel of silver per month interest. The second text also records an interest payment to be made on a sum owed by Itti-Marduk-balatu son of Nabu-ahhe-iddin to Marduk-šum-usur son of Aplaya. This tablet belongs to the archive of the Egibi family in Babylon, but was written up in Humadešu, in western Iran.

In the Babylonian documents the name of Bardiya is rendered as 'Barziya'. In the first text he is given the proper Babylonian royal title, 'king of Babylon, king of lands'. The second text merely refers to him as 'king of lands', but it shows that Bardiya was accepted as king by 14 April 522. The difficulty is to decide to what extent Bardiya could have established himself as king by that date, because Cambyses died after 1 July 522 according to DB I: §11 (**35**). Since 1 July 522 is the official date of Bardiya's acceptance as king of Persia, Bardiya could have rebelled in Persia in the spring (March) of 522; the revolt could have spread to Babylon by April 522. At Cambyses' death, Bardiya then officially declared himself king of Persia.

Part II. The Persian Empire under the first three Achaemenid Kings

2.1. DARIUS I
Seal and inscription of Darius

4. Impression of Darius' seal from Egypt

43   I am Darius, the King

SDa, Schmitt 1981

The crystal cylinder, 3.3 cm high, was found in Egypt and is now in the British Museum (BM 89132). The trilingual inscription is written in Elamite, Babylonian and Old Persian. The name 'Darius' derives from Old Persian '*Dārayavauš*' (Elam. *Dariyamauš*), and means 'He who preserves the Good'. The image shows the king in a chariot, aiming his bow at a lion, which is standing upright in front of the chariot. One animal is lying dead on the ground. The scene is flanked by palm trees. Above the hunting scene appears a winged disc with the figure of Ahura Mazda, the symbol of Achaemenid power. In depicting the king during a royal hunt, this scene, which is crafted in the traditional court style of the Achaemenid kings, not only shows the importance of the royal hunt as an expression of kingship, but is also a symbol of the power of the Persian king against his adversaries.

The Bisitun Inscription (DB)
The Old Persian text of the Bisitun Inscription was first copied by H.C. Rawlinson in 1835–37 and 1844–47; it was published in 1847. The Babylonian version was published four years later, in 1851. L.W. King and R.C. Thompson published the Elamite version in 1907. It is the most important text for the study of the history of the ancient Near East, since this trilingual inscription, written in Elamite, Babylonian and Old Persian, made it possible to decipher cuneiform writing.

The inscription together with a relief were cut on the cliff face of Mount Bisitun in northwest Iran, on the Royal Road (see **181-183**) which ran from Babylon to Ecbatana. 'Bisitun', or Behistun, derives from the OP word *Baga-stāna-* and means 'place of the gods'. Mountains, as well as rivers, were regarded as sacred by

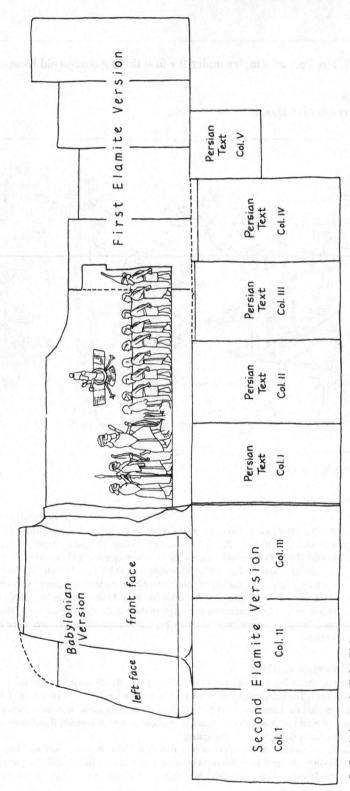

5a. Inscriptions and relief at Bisitun

5b. Inscription and relief at Bisitun

the Persians and the Elamites before them (see below **192**). It is possible that the remains of a Median fortress, which were found on the slope of the mountain, are those of the fortress Sikayuvatiš, where the rebel Gaumata was killed by Darius and the six Persian nobles.

The inscription and relief were put up some 66m above the ground. The relief itself measures 5.5 metres by 3 metres. The figure of Darius is life-size, measuring 1.72 metres, while the other figures are carved smaller, measuring 1.17 metres in height. The inscription is written in three languages, Elamite, Babylonian and Old Persian, which are arranged in columns on the rock surface. The first Elamite version is inscribed in four columns to the right of the relief, the Babylonian text to the left. The Old Persian version was written after the completion of the relief, which means after 520. It was arranged in four columns below the relief. The first Elamite version had to be rewritten because the figure of Skunkha, the Scythian rebel, was added after the relief and inscription had been set up. The relief depicts Darius standing before the nine rebels who are bound at the neck by a rope, their hands tied behind their backs. Gaumata, the usurper to the throne, lies beneath Darius' foot. The names of the rebels are all carved into the relief. Behind Darius are two Persian nobles, the King's Bow-bearer and the King's Spear-bearer.

In the Bisitun Inscription Darius recorded the events leading up to his securing the Persian throne for himself. The crucial moment for his succession was the revolt of Gaumata and his subsequent overthrow by Darius and a group of six Persian nobles. However, Darius' accession triggered a number of rebellions across the empire, which were quashed in nineteen battles fought by the army loyal to Darius. The nine rebels involved were all killed after they had been mutilated, as was customary for those who were disloyal to the king. Although the Bisitun Inscription is a vital primary source for the history of Achaemenid Persia, it is also skilful political propaganda, which served to legitimise the reign of Darius I.

44   Column I

§1. I (am) Darius, the Great King, king of kings, king of Persia, king of lands, the son of Hystaspes (OP *Vitāspa*, Elam. *Mištašpa*), the grandson of Arsames, an Achaemenid.

§2. Darius the king says: 'My father (is) Hystaspes; the father of Hystaspes (is) Arsames; the father of Arsames (is) Ariaramnes; the father of Ariaramnes (is) Teispes (OP *Cišpiš*, Elam. *Zišpiš*), the father of Teispes (is) Achaemenes (OP *Haxāmaniš*, Elam. *Hakkamannuš*).'

§3. Darius the king says: 'For that reason we are called Achaemenids. From ancient times we are noble men. From ancient times our family has been royal.'

§4. Darius the king says: '(There are) eight in my family who formerly have been kings. I (am) the ninth (king). Thus we are nine kings in succession.'

§5. Darius the king says : 'By the favour of Ahura Mazda I am king. Ahura Mazda bestowed kingship upon me.'

§6. Darius the king says: 'These (are) the countries which belong to me. By the favour of Ahura Mazda I was their king: Persia, Elam, Babylonia, Assyria, Arabia, Egypt, (the People)-by-the-Sea, Lydia, Ionia, Media, Armenia, Cappadocia, Parthia, Drangiana, Aria, Chorasmia, Bactria, Sogdiana, Gandara, Scythia, Sattagydia, Arachosia, and Maka, altogether twenty-three countries.'

§7. Darius the king says: 'These (are) the countries which belong to me. By the favour of Ahura Mazda they were my subjects; they brought tribute (OP *bāji*, Elam. *baziš*) to me. What I said to them, either by night or by day, that they used to do.'

§8. Darius the king says: 'In these countries, the man who was loyal, I treated well, who was disloyal, I punished severely. By the favour of Ahura Mazda, these countries obeyed my law. As I said to them, thus they used to do.'

§9. Darius the king says: 'Ahura Mazda bestowed this kingdom upon me. Ahura Mazda brought me aid until I had held together this kingdom. By the favour of Ahura Mazda I hold this kingship.'

(§§10–15: see above **30, 35**)

§1: Darius' royal titulature includes a reference to his ancestors, Hystaspes and Arsames. His father Hystaspes was stationed in Parthia (see §35 below). According to Herodotus, he was satrap of Persia (**38**) and had served under Cyrus II (Hdt.1.209.1–3). Nothing is known of Darius' grandfather Arsames (see **3** above).

§§2–4: In Darius' genealogy the common ancestors with the family of Cyrus are Teispes, known from the seal of Cyrus I (PFS 93, **1**), and Achaemenes, the eponymous founder of the empire, mentioned here for the first time. Taking Darius' genealogy into account, the Achaemenid king-list looks like the following:

Achaemenes	
Teispes	
Cyrus I	Ariaramnes
Cambyses I	Arsames
Cyrus II	Hystaspes
Cambyses II	Darius I
Bardiya	

Darius' genealogy and his claim that his family had always exercised kingship has been vexing scholars over several decades. The main problem is his claim to be the ninth king of the Achaemenid house, because whichever way one looks at the list of kings, Darius could either be the sixth, following his own list of his father's ancestors back to Achaemenes, or the tenth, if he counted the kings from Cyrus I to Cambyses II. He even could be the eleventh, if we include the six months' reign of Bardiya. The names of Cyrus I and his descendants are suspiciously absent from Darius' list, and their omission cannot easily be explained, except by considering that Darius had a reason to play down their role in his succession to the throne. That reason is found in the fact that Darius was not a member of the royal house and that his succession to the throne was therefore not legitimate.

Near Eastern sources testify without a doubt that Cyrus I was king of Anshan/Parsa, and that this kingship was passed down to Cyrus II. Both Cyrus I and Cyrus II name Teispes as king as well as their oldest ancestor. Cambyses II succeeded his father in 530, bearing the royal title 'king of Babylon, king of lands'. In contrast, none of Darius' ancestors held a kingship. His father Hystaspes had served under Cyrus II, while Darius himself, who had been too young to serve under Cyrus II, became one of Cambyses' spear-bearers (Gr. *doruphoros*) in Egypt (Hdt.3.139.2). While it is thus clear that Darius did not descend from a family of kings, we must also be doubtful of his claim of a common ancestor, Teispes, and especially of the existence of the eponymous founder of the empire, Achaemenes. No evidence allows us to assume that Achaemenes was ever a historical figure, or that a familial link between the family of Cyrus I and Darius I existed. This could be simply a stratagem on the part of Darius to legitimate his succession to the throne in 522, when, after the death of Cambyses II and his brother Bardiya, and in the absence of a son and heir to the throne, the line of the first Persian kings had effectively come to an end, and this political vacuum was filled by Darius. To legitimate his succession to the throne he linked his family tree to Teispes and 'created' a common ancestor, Achaemenes, in his attempt to establish the Achaemenid dynasty.

§5: Ahura Mazda: The principal god of the Achaemenid kings is attested in documents from the reign of Darius I onwards. Ahura Mazda was the 'Wise Lord', or the 'Great God, the greatest of the gods', who had created the world. To follow Ahura Mazda meant to follow the right path, to act justly and be morally good, and to speak the truth. In contrast, to follow the Lie meant to do wrong, to act unjustly and immorally, and to speak falsely. The dualistic religion had been transmitted through a prophet, Zoroaster, and was later known as Zoroastrianism. In the Bisitun Inscription Darius repeatedly stresses Ahura Mazda's support for his succession to the throne and the defeat of his enemies. However, other gods were also respected in Persian religion (see §§62-3 below, **104, 192–194**)

§6–7: Darius' list of 23 countries comprising the Persian empire, begins with two core lands, Persia and Elam. Then the order roughly follows the map in a clockwise fashion, first referring to the western provinces or satrapies, then those in the northern part, followed by the lands in the east of the empire. As his subject lands, they were obliged to pay tribute to the king or bring gifts. Only the Persians were exempt from this rule, paying taxes to the king instead (see **136–139**)

Column I (*continued*)

§16. Darius the king says: 'When I had slain Gaumata the *magus*, (there was) one man, Açina by name, the son of Upadarama; he rose up in Elam. He said to the people: "I am king in Elam." Afterwards the Elamites became rebellious (and) went (over) to Açina. He became king in Elam. And there was one man, a Babylonian, Nidintu-Bel by name, the son of Ainaira. He rose up in Babylonia. He lied to the people thus: "I am Nebuchadnezzar son of Nabonidus." Afterwards all the Babylonian people went (over) to Nidintu-Bel. Babylonia became rebellious, (and) he seized the kingship in Babylonia.'

§17. Darius the king says: 'Afterwards I sent (a messenger) to Elam. Açina was led to me bound. I slew him.'

§18. Darius the king says: 'Afterwards I went to Babylonia against Nidintu-Bel who called himself Nebuchadnezzar. The army of Nidintu-Bel held (the bank of) the Tigris. There it took its stand, and because of the waters (the river) was unpassable. Afterwards I embarked (part of) my army upon (rafts of) skin, another (part) I made ride on camels, and for another part I brought up horses. Ahura Mazda brought me aid. By the favour of Ahura Mazda we crossed the Tigris. There I defeated that army of Nidintu-Bel utterly; in the month Açiyadiya (Bab. *Kislimu*), twenty-six days had passed (*13 December 522*), then we fought the battle.'

§19. Darius the king says: 'Afterwards I went to Babylon. When I had not yet reached Babylon - (there is) a place, Zazana by name, on the Euphrates - there that Nidintu-Bel who called himself Nebuchadnezzar came with an army to fight a battle against me. Afterwards we fought the battle. Ahura Mazda brought me aid. By the favour of Ahura Mazda I defeated the army of Nidintu-Bel utterly. The rest (of the army) was thrown into the water, (and) the water carried it away. In the month Anamaka (Bab. *Tebetu*) two days had passed (*18 December 522*), then we fought the battle.'

Column II

§20. Darius the king says: 'Afterwards Nidintu-Bel fled with a few horsemen (and) went to Babylon. After that I went to Babylon. By the favour of Ahura Mazda I seized Babylon and captured Nidintu-Bel. Afterwards I slew that Nidintu-Bel in Babylon (*Babylonian text continues* [hereafter: *Bab. cont.*] and the nobles who were with him. I executed 49. This is what I did in Babylon.)'

§21. Darius the king says: 'While I was in Babylon, these (are) the countries which became rebellious from me: Persia, Elam, Media, Assyria, Egypt, Parthia, Margiana, Sattagydia, (and) Scythia.'

§22. Darius the king says: '(There was) one man, Martiya by name, the son of Cincakhri, (and there is) a place Kuganaka by name, in Persia, there he lived. He rose up in Elam. He said to the people: "I am Imaniš, king of Elam."'

§23. Darius the king says: 'At that time I was near to Elam; afterwards the Elamites were afraid of me. They captured that Martiya who was their chief and slew him.'

§24. Darius the king says: '(There was) one man, Phraortes by name, a Mede, who rose up in Media. He said to the people: "I am Khšathrita, of the family of Cyaxares." After that the Median army that was in the palace became rebellious against me (and) went (over) to Phraortes. He became king in Media.'

§25. Darius the king says: 'The Persian and Median army which was under my control was a small force. After that I sent forth an army. (There was) a Persian, Hydarnes (OP *Vidarna*, Elam. *Mitarna*) by name, my subject - him I made their chief. I said to them: "Go forth, defeat that Median army which does not call itself mine!" Afterwards Hydarnes marched off with the army. When he had come to

Media, there is a place, Maru by name, in Media, there he fought a battle with the Medes. He who was chief among the Medes was not there at the time. Ahura Mazda brought me aid. By the favour of Ahura Mazda my army defeated that rebellious army utterly. In the month Anamaka twenty-seven days had passed (*12 January 521*), then the battle was fought by them. (*Bab. cont.*: They killed ⌈ 3,827 ⌉ among them and took prisoner 4,329. Then Hydarnes did not undertake another campaign against Media.) Afterwards that army of mine waited for me in a district of Media called Kampanda until I came to Media. (*Bab. cont.*: Then they came to me at Ecbatana.)'

§26. Darius the king says: 'I sent an Armenian subject of mine, Dadaršiš by name, to Armenia. I said to him: "Go forth, defeat the rebellious army which does not call itself mine—defeat it!" Afterwards Dadaršiš marched off. When he arrived in Armenia, the rebels assembled (and) went forth to fight a battle against Dadaršiš. (There is) a village, Zuzahya by name, in Armenia, there they fought the battle. Ahura Mazda brought me aid. By the favour of Ahura Mazda my army defeated that rebellious army utterly. In the month Thuravahara (Bab. *Ayyaru*) eight days had passed (*20 May 521*), then the battle was fought by them.'

§27. Darius the king says: 'For the second time the rebels assembled and went forth to fight a battle against Dadaršiš. (There is) a fortress, Tigra by name, in Armenia, there they fought the battle. Ahura Mazda brought me aid. By the favour of Ahura Mazda my army defeated the rebellious army utterly. In the month Thuravahara eighteen days had passed (*30 May 521*), then the battle was fought by them. (*Bab. cont.*: They killed 546 among them and took prisoner 520.)'

§28. Darius the king says: 'For the third time the rebels assembled (and) went forth to fight a battle against Dadaršiš. (There is) a fortress, Uyava by name, in Armenia, there they fought the battle. Ahura Mazda brought me aid. By the favour of Ahura Mazda my army defeated that rebellious army utterly. In the month Thaigraciš (Bab. *Simannu*) nine days had passed (*20 June 521*), then the battle was fought by them. (*Bab. cont.*: They killed 472 of them and took prisoner 525(?) Then Dadaršiš did not undertake another expedition.) After that Dadaršiš waited for me until I came to Media.'

§29. Darius the king proclaims: '(There is) a Persian, Omises (OP *Vaumisa*, Elam. *Maumišša*) by name, my subject, him I sent to Armenia. I said to him: "Go forth, there is an army which is rebellious and does not call itself mine—defeat it!" Afterwards Omises marched off. When he had come to Armenia, the rebels assembled (and) went forth to fight a battle against Omises. (There is) a district, Izala by name, in Assyria, there they fought the battle. Ahura Mazda brought me aid. By the favour of Ahura Mazda my army defeated that rebellious army utterly. In the month Anamaka fifteen days had passed (*31 December 522*), then the battle was fought by them. (*Bab. cont.*: They killed 2,034 of them.)'

§30. Darius the king says: 'For the second time the rebels assembled (and) went forth to fight a battle against Omises. (There is) a district Autiyara by name, in Armenia, there they fought the battle. Ahura Mazda brought me aid. By the favour of Ahura Mazda my army defeated that rebellious army utterly. In the month Thuravahara, on the last day (*11 June 521*), the battle was fought by them. (*Bab. cont.*: They killed 2,045 among them and took prisoner 1,558. Then Omises did not undertake another expedition.) After that Omises waited for me in Armenia, until I came to Media.'

§31 Darius the king says: 'Afterwards I went away from Babylon (and) went to Media. When I had come to Media, (there is) a place, Kunduru by name, in Media, there that Phraortes who called himself king in Media came with an army to fight a battle against me. Afterwards we fought the battle. Ahura Mazda brought me aid. By the favour of Ahura Mazda I defeated the army of Phraortes utterly. In the month Adukani twenty-five days had passed (*8 May 521*), then we fought the battle. (*Bab. cont.*: We killed ⌈ 34,425?⌉ of them and took prisoner (...).)'

§32. Darius the king says: 'Afterwards Phraortes fled with a few horsemen. (There is) a district in Media, Raga by name, there he went. After that I sent an army in pursuit. Phraortes was seized (and) led to me. I cut off his nose, ears and tongue, and I put out one of his eyes. At my gate he was kept bound (and) all the people looked at him. After that I impaled him at Ecbatana. And in the fortress at Ecbatana I hanged the men who were his foremost followers. (*Bab. cont.*: I executed his nobles, a total of ⌈ 47 ⌉. I hung their heads inside Ecbatana from the battlements of the fortress.) '

§33. Darius the king says: '(There was) one man, Tritantaechmes (OP *Ciçantaxma*, Elam. *Ziššantakma*) by name, a Sagartian, who became rebellious against me. He said to the people thus: "I am king of Sagartia, of the family of Cyarxares." After that I sent forth a Persian and Median army. (There was) a Mede, Takhmaspada by name, my subject, him I made their chief. I said to them: "Go forth, defeat the rebellious army which will not call itself mine!" Afterwards Takhmaspada marched off with the army, and he fought a battle with Tritantaechmes. Ahura Mazda brought me aid. By the favour of Ahura Mazda my army defeated the rebellious army and it captured Tritantaechmes (and) led (him) to me. After that I cut off his nose and ears, and I put out one of his eyes. At my gate he was kept bound (and) all the people looked at him. Afterwards I impaled him at Arbela. (*Bab. cont.*: The total dead and surviving of the rebel force was ⌈ 447?⌉ .)'

§34. Darius the king says: 'This (is) what I have done in Media.'

§35. Darius the king says: 'Parthia and Hyrcania rebelled against me. They called themselves supporters of Phraortes. My father Hystaspes was in Parthia - the people had abandoned him; they had become rebellious. After that Hystaspes marched off with the army which was faithful to him. (There is) a place, Vishpauzatiš by name, in Parthia, there he fought a battle with the Parthians. Ahura Mazda brought me aid. By the favour of Ahura Mazda Hystaspes defeated that rebellious army utterly. In the month Viyaxna twenty-two days had passed (*8 March 521*), then the battle was fought by them. (*Bab. cont.*: They killed ⌈ 6,346 ⌉ of them and took prisoner ⌈ 4,346?⌉ .)'

Column III

§36. Darius the king says: 'Afterwards I sent forth a Persian army to Hystaspes from Raga. When that army had reached Hystaspes, he took it (under his command and) marched off. (There is) a place, Patigrabana by name, in Parthia, there he fought a battle with the rebels. Ahura Mazda brought me aid. By the favour of Ahura Mazda Hystaspes defeated the rebellious army utterly. In the month Garmapada one day had passed (*11 July 521*), then the battle was fought by them. (*Bab. cont.*: They killed 6,570 of them and took prisoner 4,192. Then he executed their leader and the nobles who were with him, a total of 80.)'

§37. Darius the king says: 'After that the country became mine. This (is) what I have done in Parthia.'

§38. Darius the king says:'(There is) a country, Margiana by name, that rebelled against me. There was one man, Frada by name, a Margian, they made him their chief. After that I sent a Persian, Dadaršiš by name, my subject, satrap of Bactria, against him. I said to him: "Go forth, defeat the army which does not call itself mine!" Afterwards Dadaršiš with the army marched off, and he fought a battle with the Margians. Ahura Mazda brought me aid. By the favour of Ahura Mazda my army defeated that rebellious army utterly. In the month Açiyadiya twenty-three days had passed (*28 December 521*), then the battle was fought by them. (*Bab. cont.*: He executed Frada and the nobles who were with him, a total of ⌐46?⌐. He killed ⌐55,2xx?⌐ and took prisoner 6,572.)'

§39. Darius the king says: 'After that the country became mine. This (is) what I have done in Bactria.'

§40. Darius the king says: '(There was) one man, Vahyazdata by name, and (at) a place, Tarava by name, (and) a district, Yutiya by name, in Persia, there he lived. He rose up in Persia a second time. He said to the people: "I am Bardiya son of Cyrus." After that, the Persian army, which was in the palace, (and which had come up) from Anshan previously, rebelled against me (and) went (over) to that Vahyazdata. He became king in Persia.'

§41. Darius the king says: 'Afterwards I sent forth the Persian and Median army which was under (my control). (There was) a Persian, Artavardiya by name, my subject, I made him their commander. The rest of the Persian army went after me to Media. Afterwards Artavardiya went with the army to Persia. When he arrived in Persia—there is a place named Rakha, in Persia—there that Vahyazdata who called himself Bardiya came with an army to fight a battle against Artavardiya. Afterwards they fought the battle. Ahura Mazda brought me aid. By the favour of Ahura Mazda my army defeated that army of Vahyazdata utterly. In the month Thuravahara twelve days had passed (*24 May 521*), then the battle was fought by them. (*Bab. cont.*: They killed 4,404 of them and took prisoner (...).)'

§42. Darius the king says: 'Afterwards Vahyazdata fled with a few horsemen (and) went to Paišiyauvada. From there he took an army to himself. Once more he marched to fight a battle against Artavardiya. There is a mountain, Parga by name, there they fought the battle. Ahura Mazda brought me aid. By the favour of Ahura Mazda my army defeated that army of Vahyazdata utterly. In the month Garmapada five days had passed (*15 July 521*), then the battle was fought by them. (*Bab. cont.*: They killed ⌐6,246⌐ of them and took prisoner ⌐4,464⌐. And (my army) captured Vahyazdata, and they captured the men who were his foremost followers.'

§43. Darius the king says: 'Afterwards I (impaled) Vahyazdata and the men who were his foremost followers. (There is) a place, Uvadaicaya by name, in Persia, there I impaled them.'

§44. Darius the king says: 'This (is) what I have done in Persia.'

§45. Darius the king says: 'That Vahyazdata who called himself Bardiya had sent forth an army to Arachosia against a Persian, Vivana by name, my subject, satrap of Arachosia, and he (*Vahyazdata*) had made one man their commander. He (*Vahyazdata*) had said to them: "Go forth and defeat Vivana and the army which calls itself (that) of Darius the king!" Afterwards the army which Vahyazdata had sent forth against Vivana marched off to fight a battle. (There is) a fortress, Kapišakaniš by name, there they fought the battle. Ahura Mazda brought me aid. By the favour of Ahura Mazda my army defeated that rebellious army utterly. In the month Anamaka thirteen days had passed (*22 December 522*), then the battle was fought by them. (*Bab. cont.*: The total dead and surviving of the troops whom Vahyazdata had sent was (...).)'

§46. Darius the king says: 'Once more the rebels assembled and went forth to fight a battle against Vivana. (There is) a district, Gandutava by name, there they fought the battle. Ahura Mazda brought me aid. By the favour of Ahura Mazda my army defeated that rebellious army utterly. In the month Viyaxna seven days had passed (*21 February 521*), then the battle was fought by them. (*Bab. cont.*: The total dead and surviving of the troops whom Vahyazdata had sent was 4,579.)'

§47. Darius the king says: 'Afterwards the commander of the army which Vahyazdata had sent forth against Vivana fled with a few horsemen and went off. (There is) a fortress, Aršada by name, in Arachosia, past that he went. Afterwards Vivana marched off with the army in pursuit of them. There he captured him, and he slew the men who were his foremost followers. (*Bab. cont.*: The total dead and surviving of the troops of Vivana was [...].)'

§48. Darius the king says: 'After that the country became mine. This (is) what I have done in Arachosia.'

§49. Darius the king says: 'Whilst I was in Persia and Media, for the second time the Babylonians rebelled against me. (There was) one man, Arakha by name, an Armenian, the son of Haldita, who rose up in Babylonia, from a district called Dubala. He lied to the people thus: "I am Nebuchadnezzar son of Nabonidus." Afterwards the Babylonian people rebelled against me (and) went (over) to that Arakha. He seized Babylon. He became king in Babylon.'

§50. Darius the king says: 'Afterwards I sent forth an army to Babylon. (There was) a Persian, Intaphernes (OP *Vindafarna*, Elam. *Mindaparna*) by name, my subject, him I made their chief. I said to them: "Go forth, defeat that Babylonian army which will not call itself mine!" Afterwards Intaphernes went to Babylon with the army. Ahura Mazda brought me aid. By the favour of Ahura Mazda Intaphernes slew the Babylonians and led (them) in fetters. In the month Varkazana twenty-two days had passed (*27 November 521*), then he captured that Arakha who falsely called himself Nebuchadnezzar, and the men who were his foremost followers, I gave orders that Arakha and the men who were his foremost followers should be impaled at Babylon. (*Bab. cont.*: The total dead and surviving of the army of Arakha was 2,497.)'

Column IV
§51. Darius the king says: 'This (is) what I have done in Babylon.'

§52. Darius the king says: 'This (is) what I have done by the favour of Ahura Mazda in one and the same year, after I became king: I have fought nineteen battles. By the favour of Ahura Mazda I defeated them and captured nine kings. One (was) a *magus*, Gaumata by name; he lied, saying: "I am Bardiya, the son of Cyrus." He made Persia rebellious. One (was) an Elamite, Açina by name, he lied, saying: "I am king in Elam." He made Elam rebellious. One (was) a Babylonian, Nidintu-Bel by name. He lied, saying: "I am Nebuchadnezzar son of Nabonidus."

He made Babylonia rebellious. One (was) a Persian, Martiya by name. He lied, saying: "I am Imaniš, king in Elam." He made Elam rebellious. One (was) a Mede, Phraortes by name; he lied, saying: "I am Khšathrita, of the family of Cyaxares." He made Media rebellious. One (was) a Sagartian, Tritantaechmes by name. He lied, saying: "I am king in Sagartia, of the family of Cyarxares." He made Sagartia rebellious. One (was) a Margian, Frada by name. He lied, saying: "I am king in Margiana." He made Margiana rebellious. One (was) a Persian, Vahyazdata by name. He lied, saying: "I am Bardiya son of Cyrus." He made Persia rebellious. One (was) an Armenian, Arakha by name. He lied, saying: "I am Nebuchadnezzar son of Nabonidus." He made Babylonia rebellious.'

§53. Darius the king says: 'These (are) the nine kings whom I have captured in these battles.'

§54. Darius the king says: 'These (are) the countries which became rebellious. The Lie made them rebellious, because these men lied to the people. Afterwards Ahura Mazda gave them into my hand. As (was) my desire, so I treated them.'

§§16–54: Following the account of the revolt of the first usurper to the Persian throne, Gaumata, the bulk of the inscription is devoted to recounting the revolts of the other eight men who proclaimed themselves king, and the nineteen battles Darius fought to secure his kingship. According to Darius, the revolts occurred as follows:

1) The revolt of Gaumata.

2) Açina revolted in Elam.

3) Nidintu-Bel revolted in Babylonia, claiming to be the son of Nabonidus. Darius defeated him twice on 13 and on 18 December 522.

4) Martiya revolted in Elam.

5) Phraortes revolted in Media. His army was defeated by Hydarnes on 12 January 521 and by the Armenian Dadaršiš (different from the Persian satrap in Column III §38) on 20 May, 30 May and 20 June. The Persian Omises also defeated rebel armies at Izala (31 December 522) and Autiyara (11 June 521). Darius himself finally defeated Phraortes on 8 May 521.

6) Tritantaechmes revolted but was defeated by Takhmaspada. Parthia and Hyrcania revolted but were defeated by Hystaspes on 8 March 521 and again on 11 July 521.

7) Frada revolted in Margiana. Defeated by Dadaršiš on 28 December 521.

8) Vahyazdata revolted in Persia. Defeated on 24 May and again on 15 July 521. Vahyazdata's army lost two more battles, on 22 December 522 and 21 February 521.

9) Arakha revolted in Babylon. Defeated by Intaphernes on 27 November 521.

Column IV (*continued*)

§55. Darius the king says: 'You who shall be king hereafter, protect yourself vigorously from the Lie. The man who follows the Lie, punish him severely, if you shall think thus: "Let my country be secure!"'

§56. Darius the king says: 'This is what I did. By the favour of Ahura Mazda in one and the same year I have done it. You who shall read this inscription hereafter, let what (has been) done by me convince you, do not consider it a lie.'

§57. Darius the king says: 'I will take Ahura Mazda's anger upon myself that I did this truly, and not falsely, in one and the same year.'

§58. Darius the king says: 'By the favour of Ahura Mazda also I have done much more that (has) not (been) written down in this inscription; for this reason (it has) not (been) written down, lest what I have done should seem (too) much to him who will read this inscription hereafter, (and) this should not convince him, (but) he regard it (as) false.'

§59. Darius the king says: 'In their entire lives, previous kings have not done so much as I, by the favour of Ahura Mazda, have done in one and the same year.'

§60. Darius the king says: 'Now let what I have done convince you! Thus make (it) known to the people, do not conceal (it)! If you shall not conceal this record, (but) make (it) known to the people, may Ahura Mazda be a friend to you. May your offspring be numerous, and may you live long!'

§61. Darius the king says: 'If you shall conceal this record (and) not make (it) known to the people, may Ahura Mazda be your destroyer and may you have no offspring!'

§62. Darius the king says: 'I did what I did in one and the same year. By the favour of Ahura Mazda I did (it). Ahura Mazda and the other gods who are brought me aid.'

§63. Darius the king says: 'For this reason Ahura Mazda and the other gods who are brought me aid because I was not disloyal, I was not a follower of the Lie. I was no evil-doer, neither I nor my family, (but) I acted according to righteousness. Neither to the powerless nor to the powerful did I do wrong, and the man who supported my (royal) house, him I treated well; the man who did it harm, him I punished severely.'

§64. Darius the king says: 'You who shall be king hereafter—the man who shall be a follower of the Lie, or (the man) who shall be an evil-doer, may you not be his friend, (but) punish him severely.'

§65. Darius the king says: 'You who shall hereafter look at this inscription which I have written down and these sculptures, do not destroy (them). As long as you have strength, protect them!'

§66. Darius the king says: 'If you look at this inscription or these sculptures (and) do not destroy them and, as long as there is strength in you, protect them, may Ahura Mazda be your friend, and may your offspring be numerous, and may you live long! And may Ahura Mazda make what you shall do successful for you!'

§67. Darius the king says: 'If you look at this inscription or these sculptures (and) destroy them and do not, as long as there is strength in you, protect them, may Ahura Mazda be your destroyer, and may you have no offspring! And may Ahura Mazda let what you shall do go wrong for you!'

§68. Darius the king says: 'These (are) the men who at that time were there, when I slew Gaumata the *magus* who called himself Bardiya. At that time these men co-operated as my followers: Intaphernes by name, the son of Vahyasparuva, a Persian; Otanes (OP *Utana,* Elam. *Huttana*) by name, son of Thukhra (Elam. *Tukkura*), a Persian; Gobryas (OP *Gaubaruva,* Elam. *Kambarna*) by name, the son of Mardonius (OP, Elam. *Marduniya*), a Persian; Hydarnes (OP *Vidarna,* Elam. *Mitarna*) by name, the son of Bagabigna, a Persian; Megabyxus (OP, Elam. *Bagabuxša*) by name, the son of Datavahya (Elam. *Daddumaniya*), a Persian; Ardumaniš (Elam. *Hardumannuš*) by name, the son of Vahuka (Elam. *Maukka* (Gr. *Ochus*)), a Persian.'

§69. Darius the king says: 'You who shall be king hereafter, protect well the offspring of these men!'

§§55–69: Darius is emphatic in stressing the truthfulness of the information he has provided about the revolts. Very likely they were indeed all quashed within the time-frame provided in the inscription, i.e., between 13 December 522 and 28 December 521. Babylonian documents attest the fact that this year had an intercalary month, dating from March 522 to April 521.

Darius is equally eager to point out the difference between right and wrong, warning anyone who reads the inscription or sees the relief not to destroy it, and cursing those who would. The importance of the social values of numerous offspring and the prosperity of the family are emphasised here.

§68: The names of the six Persians who supported Darius in his claim for the throne correspond, with the exception of the last name, with the names supplied in Herodotus (Hdt.3.70, **38**). Vindafarna son of Vahyaparuva is Intaphernes; Utana son of Thukhra, is Otanes son of Pharnaspes; Gaubaruva son of Marduniya is Gobryas son of Mardonius; Vidarna son of Bagabigna is Hydarnes son of Megabazus; Bagabuxša son of Datavahya is Megabyxus. Ardumaniš son of Vahuka is replaced in Herodotus by a Persian called Aspathines. Ardumaniš is thought to have died at some time during Darius' reign, and possibly was replaced by Aspathines, who appears alongside Gobryas on the relief and in the inscriptions of Darius' tomb at Naqš-e Rustam (see below **113–115**). Altogether, Herodotus' list of the names of the Persian nobles thus reflects an accurate source, except for the incompatibility between the name given to Otanes' father in Old Persian as Thukhra and as Pharnaspes in Herodotus.

Column IV (*continued*)

§70. Darius the king says: 'By the favour of Ahura Mazda this (is) the inscription which I have made besides in Aryan. It has been written both on clay tablets and on parchment. I also wrote down my name and my lineage, and it was written down and was read (aloud) before me. Afterwards I have sent this inscription in all directions among the lands. The people strove (to use it).'

§70: This paragraph is essential for the understanding of the inscription itself, though this part of the text had not been read or restored by Rawlinson, and could only partially be read by King and Thompson. The present reading relies on restorations to the text based on a squeeze of the inscription made by Cameron in 1951. The paragraph was included in the Elamite and Old Persian versions, but was omitted in the Babylonian text.

The important information revealed in this paragraph is the fact that Darius ordered a new form of writing to be created. This was the cuneiform script which we now call Old Persian, used to record a dialect of Old Iranian. Introduced here for the first time, the use of the Old Persian script was limited to the royal inscriptions of the Achaemenids.

The paragraph also indicates that copies of the Bisitun Inscription were distributed throughout the empire. What has come down to us from those copies is one text written in Aramaic, which was found in Elephantine in Egypt, and is in fact a late copy, dating to 420. Fragments of a copy written in Babylonian cuneiform were found in Babylon. Further archaeological evidence suggests that the relief accompanying the Bisitun Inscription was also copied alongside the Babylonian copy. It has been suggested that versions of the text were written in other languages spoken within the empire, including Greek, but if these did exist, they were written on perishable material and did not survive.

Column V

§71. Darius the king says: 'This (is) what I did in the second and the third year, after I became king. (There is) a country called Elam that became rebellious. (There was) one man, Athamaita by name, an Elamite. They made him (their) chief. After that I sent forth an army. (There was) one man, Gobryas by name, a Persian, my subject, I made him their chief. Afterwards Gobryas went with the army to Elam and fought a battle with the Elamites. Afterwards Gobryas defeated the Elamites and crushed (them); he captured their chief and led him to me. After that I slew him. After that the country became mine.'

§72. Darius the king says: 'Those Elamites were disloyal, and Ahura Mazda was not worshipped by them. I worshipped Ahura Mazda. By the favour of Ahura Mazda, as (was) my desire, so I treated them.'

§73. Darius the king says: 'He who worships Ahura Mazda shall have the (fulfilment of his) prayer, both (while he is) living and (when he is) dead.'

§74. Darius the king says: 'Afterwards I went with an army against Scythia. After that the Scythians who wear the pointed cap came against me, when I arrived at the sea. By means of rafts (of skin) I crossed it with the whole army. Afterwards I defeated those Scythians utterly. They (*the army*) captured another part of them (*Scythians*); that (part) was led to me bound. And they captured their chief,

Skunkha by name, (and) led him to me bound. There I made another (their) chief, as was my desire. After that the country became mine.'

§75. Darius the king says: 'Those Scythians were disloyal, and Ahura Mazda was not worshipped by them. I, however, worshipped Ahura Mazda. By the favour of Ahura Mazda, as (was) my desire, so I treated them.'

§76. Darius the king says: 'He who worships Ahura Mazda shall have the (fulfilment of his) prayer, both (while he is) living and (when he is) dead.'

Kent 1953; Schmitt 1991; Vallat 1977; von Voigtlander 1978

§§71–6: In this column Darius adds two additional revolts, one in Elam and one in Scythia, which must have occurred later than those he recorded in his main account.

Darius' Foundation Charter from Susa

45   §1. Ahura Mazda is a great god, who created this earth, who created the sky, who created man, who created happiness for man, who made Darius king, one king among many, one lord among many.

§2. I am Darius, the Great King, the king of kings, king of the lands, king of this earth, son of Hystaspes, an Achaemenid. And Darius the king says: 'Ahura Mazda, who is the greatest of the gods, has created me, has made me king, has given me this kingdom, which is great, and which has good horses and good men. By the favour of Ahura Mazda, my father Hystaspes and Arsames, my grandfather, were both alive when Ahura Mazda made me king on this earth. Thus it was the desire of Ahura Mazda to choose me as his man on this entire earth, he made me king on this earth. I worshipped Ahura Mazda. Ahura Mazda brought me aid. What I ordered (to be done), this he accomplished for me. I achieved all of what I did by the grace of Ahura Mazda.

§3. 'This palace which I built at Susa: its materials were brought from afar. The earth was dug down deep, until the rock was reached in the earth. When the excavation had been made, then rubble was packed down, some 40 cubits (*c.20 m*) deep, another (part) 20 cubits deep. On that rubble the palace was constructed. And that earth, which was dug deep, and that rubble, which was packed down, and the sun-dried bricks, which were moulded, the Babylonian people - they performed (these tasks).

§4. 'The cedar timber was brought from a mountain called Lebanon. The Assyrian people brought it to Babylon. From Babylon the Carians and Ionians brought it to Susa. The sissoo-timber was brought from Gandara and from Carmania. The gold which was worked here was brought from Sardis and from Bactria. The precious stone lapis lazuli and carnelian which was worked here was brought from Sogdiana. The precious stone turquoise, which was worked here, this was brought from Chorasmia. The silver and the ebony were brought from Egypt. The ornamentation with which the wall was adorned was brought from Ionia. The ivory which was worked here was brought from Ethiopia, and from India and from Arachosia. The stone columns which were worked here were brought from a village called Abiradu, in Elam. The stone-cutters who worked the stone were Ionians and Sardians. The goldsmiths who worked the gold were Medes and Egyptians. The men who worked the wood were Sardians and Egyptians. The men who worked the baked brick were Babylonians. The men who adorned the wall were Medes and Egyptians.'

§5. Darius the king says: 'At Susa a very excellent work was ordered, a very excellent work was brought to completion. May Ahura Mazda protect me, and Hystaspes my father and my country.'

DSf; Grillot-Susini 1990

This so-called Foundation Charter from Susa was first published in 1929. The trilingual inscription is written in Elamite, Babylonian and Old Persian. Copies of this text were found written on clay and on marble tablets, as well as on the glazed tiles of the frieze of the Great Hall. The inscription is now in the Louvre; fragments are in the Archaeological Museum in Susa. Two further foundation charters, one written in Elamite (DSz) and one in Babylonian (DSaa), were found in the Apadana, the Throne-Hall, of Darius I during the excavation season of 1969/70, and are thought to be variants of the above text.

The text is arranged in the standard style of Achaemenid royal inscriptions. The invocation of Ahura Mazda, affirming that the king acts through his divine support, is followed by the king's genealogy. The genesis in the first paragraph proclaims Ahura Mazda as the creator of the world and the creator of man. As in the Bisitun Inscription, Darius emphasises that his kingship has the support and approval of Ahura Mazda. The reference to the 'good horses and good men' provides an insight into the values of Persian society, that is, the importance of horses and horse-breeding (see **104** §2), and the recognition of the value of good men. This could be a reference to good soldiers, but in the context of the foundation text, which has no military reference, the term 'good men' refers more generally to the peoples of the empire who are loyal subjects of the Persian king.

The third part provides information on the materials which were used for the building of the palace. These precious materials were brought from all over the Persian empire, from Egypt in the west to Bactria in the east. Likewise, the workers and artisans were selected from different parts of the empire, according to their expertise. Archaeology has established that Ionian stone-masons were employed to build Cyrus' palace in Pasargadae, as well as by Darius at Susa and at Persepolis.

The building of Darius' palace at Susa probably began very soon after Darius became king, probably as early as 520. Darius may have wanted to lay claim to the former Elamite capital. To some extent he thereby made a statement of his political claim to succeed to the throne of the previous Elamite and Persian kings.

Inscription from Susa

46   §1. Ahura Mazda is a great god, who created this earth, who created the sky, who created man, who created happiness for man, who made Darius king, one king of many, one lord of many.

§2. I am Darius, the Great King, king of kings, king of lands containing many men, king of this great earth far and wide, son of Hystaspes, an Achaemenid, a Persian, son of a Persian, an Aryan, having Aryan lineage.

§3. Darius the king says: 'By the favour of Ahura Mazda these are the countries which I seized outside Persia: I ruled over them, they brought me tribute. They did what I told them. My law held them firm. Media, Elam, Parthia, Aria, Bactria, Sogdiana, Chorasmia, Drangiana, Arachosia, Sattagydia, Gandara, Sind, Amyrgian Scythians, Scythians with pointed caps, Babylonia, Assyria, Arabia, Egypt, Armenia, Cappadocia, Sardis, Ionia, Scythians from Across-the-Sea (*Black Sea*), Skudra, *petasos*-wearing Ionians, Libyans, Ethiopians, men from Maka, Carians.'

§4. Darius the king says: 'I changed many bad things that had been done to good things. By the favour of Ahura Mazda I dealt with the countries which fought against each other, where peoples were killing each other, so that their people do not kill each other any more, and I returned everyone to his place. And in the face of my decisions, they respected them in such a way that the strong neither beats nor deprives the weak.'

§5. Darius the king says: By the favour of Ahura Mazda, I completed many building projects which previously had been abandoned. I saw that the fortification walls (of Susa), which had been built previously, had fallen into disrepair from age, and I rebuilt them. These are the fortification walls which I rebuilt.'

§6. Darius the king says: 'May Ahura Mazda together with the (other) gods protect me, and my royal house, and what has been inscribed by me.'

DSe

§§1–2: The text begins with the standard formula found in the royal Persian inscriptions, the invocation of the god Ahura Mazda and the lineage of the king. Following his list of royal titles, Darius states his lineage as an Achaemenid, a Persian, and an Aryan. He thus gives first the clan (Achaemenid), then his tribe (Persian), and his ethnic origin (Aryan). The latter defines the peoples who are linked through a common language, Aryan.

§3: In his lists of lands, Darius names twenty-nine lands of his empire. Absent from the list is Persis, because only those countries which pay tribute to the king are mentioned. Persis was exempt from paying tribute, but was obliged to pay taxes (see below **136–139**). This list of lands is identical to the one given in his inscription at Naqš-e Rustam (see below **48**). The *petasos* worn by the Ionians was a particular type of felt hat.

§4: It is unclear which problems Darius is referring to in this inscription, but in all likelihood he is referring to the revolts which shook the Persian empire immediately after his accession to the throne in September 522. Darius portrays himself as the king who imposed order on the upheavals and whose law was respected by everyone.

§5: Here we see a reflection of the notion that the good rule of a king is also expressed in his building works. In his public image the king regards himself as the ruler who observes the law and ensures peace among his peoples. This peace within the empire is manifest in the construction work ordered by the king. The last paragraph stresses again the importance of the written word (see **44**:III §70), implying that those sentiments which the king has ordered to be put in writing should have everlasting value.

Inscription from Mount Elvand

47   §1. Ahura Mazda is a great god, who created this earth, who created that sky, who created man, who created happiness for man, who made Darius king, one king of many, one lord of many.

§2. I am Darius, the Great King, king of kings, king of lands containing many men, king of this great earth far and wide, son of Hystaspes, an Achaemenid.

DE

This inscription was carved in a niche carved into the rock face of Mount Elvand some 12 km southwest of Ecbatana/Hamadan. It was written in three languages, Elamite, Babylonian and Old Persian. It is similar to a second text next to it mentioning Xerxes (see **65**), and it has been suggested that both inscriptions were carved on Xerxes' order. They both include the first two paragraphs of Achaemenid royal inscriptions, the invocation of Ahura Mazda as the protector of the Achaemenid royal house, and the royal titles of the Persian king. The inscriptions were carved at a place which was passed by travellers on their way through the mountains.

First inscription from Naqš-e Rustam

Naqš-e Rustam, about 6 km north of Persepolis, is the burial site of four Achaemenid kings, where four cross-shaped tombs were cut into the rock face of the Hossein Kuh. The tombs are those of Darius I, Xerxes, Artaxerxes I and Darius II, and their façades are all identical, with a relief cut in the top part of the cross-shape. Each relief depicts the king in front of a fire altar and an incense-burner (see on **199**). This scene is placed on a huge throne or platform, which is carried by human figures, each one individually carved and representing one of the lands of the empire. Only the tomb of Darius I bears any inscriptions. DNa (**48**) is inscribed behind the figure of the king, DNb (**103**) is inscribed on both sides of the door in the centre of the cross-beam; both are written in Elamite, Babylonian and Old Persian.

48   (§§1–3 = **46**)

§4. Darius the king says: 'When Ahura Mazda saw this earth in commotion, he thereafter bestowed it upon me, he made me king. I am king. By the favour of Ahura Mazda I subdued it; they did what I said, as was my desire. If now you should think "How many are the countries which Darius the king held?", look at the sculptures of those who bear the throne, then you will know. Then it will become known to you: the spear of a Persian man has gone far. Then shall it become known to you: a Persian man has given battle far indeed from Persia.'

§5. Darius the king says: 'That which has been done, all that I did by the will of Ahura Mazda. Ahura Mazda brought me aid, until I had done the work. May Ahura Mazda protect me from harm, and my royal house, and this land. This I pray of Ahura Mazda, this may Ahura Mazda give me.

§6. 'O man, that which is the command of Ahura Mazda, let it not seem repugnant to you. Do not leave the right path, do not rise in rebellion!'

DNa

6. Tomb façade at Naqš-e Rustam

While §§1–3 are identical with the first three paragraphs of the inscription from Susa (**46**), §4 emphasises the importance of the congruence of the relief and the inscription. With reference again to the revolts of 522/1, Darius repeats his claim, already made in the inscription from Susa, that all lands of the empire have been brought under his control and are now loyal to him. The powerful image of the peoples of the empire bearing the throne of the Persian king symbolises the unity which Darius claims to have achieved. The statement 'the spear of a Persian man has gone far' means that the army of the Persian king has succeeded in quashing the rebellions and securing the lands for the empire.

Darius and Egypt
Inscription of Darius' statue from Heliopolis, found in Susa

49   §1. Ahura Mazda is a great god, who created this earth, who created that sky, who created man, who created happiness for man, who made Darius king. Here is the statue made of stone which Darius had ordered to be made in Egypt, so that he who sees it in the future may know that the Persian man held Egypt.

§2. I am Darius, the Great King, king of kings, king of lands, king over this great earth, the son of Hystaspes, the Achaemenid. Darius the king says: 'May Ahura Mazda protect me and that which I have made!'

DSab

The statue of Darius was found during excavations in Susa in 1972. It was probably brought from Heliopolis in Egypt to Susa, and may have been one of a pair. The complete statue (the head is unfortunately missing) probably measured about three metres in height. Darius is shown wearing Persian dress, but the rigid style of the

7. Darius' statue from Susa

sculpture is Egyptian. The missing head would not have been a portrait. The statue is now in the Archaeological Museum in Tehran in Iran. The trilingual inscription is written on the left side of Darius' robe. This is the only free-standing statue we have from the Achaemenid period. The text acknowledges Darius as king of Egypt.

Hieroglyphic inscription on the base of Darius' statue from Susa

50 (...) The strong King, great in his powers, lord of strength like Him who presides in Letopolis, lord of his own hand, who conquers the Nine Bows, excellent in counsel, outstanding in his plans, lord of the curved sword, when he penetrates the mass (of the enemy), shooting at the target without his arrow missing (it), whose strength is like that of (the god) Montu.

The King of Upper and Lower Egypt, Lord of the Two Lands, Darius, ever-living! The Great King, king of kings, the supreme lord of (all) the lands, (son of) the god's father, Hystaspes, the Achaemenid, who has appeared as king of Upper and Lower Egypt on the seat where Horus rules over the living, like Re, the first of the gods, forever.

Yoyotte 1974

The hieroglyphic inscription was carved in five columns onto the base of the statue of Darius. Darius is addressed with the royal titles appropriate for an Egyptian pharaoh, followed in the second paragraph by the standard Achaemenid royal titulature. The Egyptian deity Montu is a god of war, appearing in the form of a falcon. Montu is the main deity of the city of Letopolis in Lower Egypt. Herodotus refers to Letopolis as Papremis, where Inaros, leader of the Egyptian revolt against Persia (see below pp.57-60), fought against Achaemenes, the son of Darius I (**84**). The 'Nine Bows' is an Egyptian name for all the people of the world. For Horus, see on **22**.

Epitaph for the Apis bull interred in 518

51 Year 4, third month of the season of Shemu, day 13 (*November 518*), of His Majesty of Upper and Lower Egypt, Darius, given life (like that of) Re (forever). This god was led in peace towards the perfect West; he was [laid to rest in the necropolis, in the place] which His Majesty has made for him - never had [such a place been made before - after all the ceremonies had been performed for him] in the Hall of Embalming. Indeed, His Majesty glorified [him] as [Horus did his father Osiris].

A great sarcophagus of monolithic precious stone was made for him, as has been done since antiquity. Sets of linen were made for him; there were brought to him his amulets and all his ornaments [of gold and all the] precious [materials], they were more beautiful than those which had been made before. Indeed, His Majesty loved [the living Apis] more than any king. The majesty of this god went forth to the sky in year 4, first month of the season of Shemu, [day 4. He was born] in year 5, first month of the season Peret, day 29, under the Majesty of the king of Upper and Lower Egypt, [Mesuti-Re (*Cambyses II*)]. He was installed in the temple of Ptah in the year [... The perfect duration of the life of] this god was 8 years, 3 months, and 5 days.

May Darius act for him (*Apis*), [as one endowed with life and prosperity forever].

In style the inscription is similar to Cambyses' epitaph for the Apis bull (**21**). The Persian king ordered a proper, lavish burial for the deceased Apis bull and a sarcophagus to be made for him. For Ptah, see on **22**.

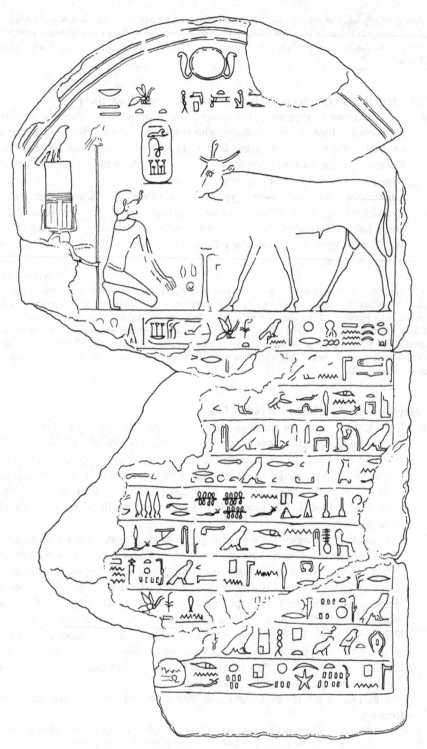

8. Darius' stele for the Apis bull

Stele from Red Sea Canal

52 §1.Ahura Mazda is a great god, who created that sky, who created this earth, who
created man, who created happiness for man, who made Darius king, who gave to
king Darius a kingdom which is great , which possesses good horses and good men.
§2. I am Darius, the Great King, king of kings, king of lands, king of this great
earth, son of Hystaspes, the Achaemenid.
§3. Darius the king says: 'I am a Persian. From Persia I seized Egypt. I ordered
the digging of this canal from a river called Nile, which flows in Egypt, to the
sea which begins in Persia. Afterwards this canal was dug just as I ordered, and
ships passed through this canal from Egypt to Persia, as I had wished.'

DZc

Darius had ordered the completion of the building of a canal leading from the Nile to the Red Sea in 517.
This project had already begun under the Egyptian king Necho (610-595), but had not been completed. The
canal was about 45 metres wide and 5 metres deep, covering a distance of 84 km. It was lined with at least
twelve stelae, set up by the order of Darius, each one over three metres high and inscribed in three cuneiform
scripts as well as in Egyptian hieroglyphic, with a text that included lists of the lands of the empire. The
canal ran from Bubastis on the Nile via modern Ismailiya to the Gulf of Suez. Four stelae have been found;
three are now in the Egyptian Museum in Cairo. The above Old Persian text from the stele from Shalluf is
the best preserved one; this stele is now in the Louvre.

Darius' claim to have seized Egypt is an expression of the *damnatio memoriae* (erasure from memory)
of Cambyses II and his achievements.

Greek evidence for the Red Sea Canal

53 [158.1] Psammetichus had a son, Necho, who became king of Egypt. He was the
first to attempt to construct a canal to the Erythraean Sea (*Red Sea*), which was
completed by Darius the Persian. Its length is a four days' voyage, and its width
allows two triremes to be rowed abreast. [158.2] It is fed by the Nile, which the
canal leaves a little above Bubastis, near Patumus, an Arabian town; it leads into
the Erythraean Sea.

Herodotus 2.158.1-2

Darius is credited with the completed construction of the canal to the Red Sea, confirmed by the primary
evidence from Egypt (**52**). Herodotus provides additional information about the length and width of the
canal. His information certainly comes from Egypt; he may even have seen the canal himself.

Hieroglyphic Inscription of Udjahorresnet

54 (...) The Majesty of the King of Upper and Lower Egypt, Darius, may he live
forever, commanded me to return to Egypt—when His Majesty was in Elam and
was the Great King of all foreign lands and Great Ruler of Egypt—in order
to restore the establishment of the House of Life [...], after it had decayed.
Foreigners carried me from foreign country to foreign country. I was delivered
to Egypt as commanded by the Lord of the Two Lands.

I did as His Majesty had commanded me. I furnished them (*the people referred
to in the lacuna above*) with all their staff, consisting of the wellborn, no lowborn
among them. I placed them in the charge of every learned man [in order to teach
them] all their work. His Majesty had commanded to give them every good thing,
in order that they might carry out all their work. I supplied them with everything
that was useful for them, and all their requirements that were in writing, as they
had been before.

His Majesty did this because he knew the worth of this craft, in making all that are sick live, in making the names of all the gods, their temples, their offerings, and the conduct of their festivals endure forever.

Lichtheim 1960: 39-40

This section of the inscription (see also above **20**) refers to political events in the empire under Darius I. According to Udjahorresnet, Darius was in Elam, when the king ordered him to return to Egypt and restore the House of Life at Saïs. This may refer to Darius' campaigns against the revolts in Elam in 522/1, following the death of Bardiya/Gaumata. It is uncertain whether Udjahorresnet was in fact accompanying the king on this campaign, but it is clear that he had left Egypt at some point early in Darius' reign. Egyptian evidence further suggests that an Egyptian named Petubastis (III) proclaimed himself king of Egypt in 522/1. As no more is known about him, it must be assumed that his attempt to seize power was curtailed by the satrap of Egypt, Aryandes.

Demotic Papyrus from Egypt

55 The affairs which occurred after those which have been written in the book of laws since year 44 of the Pharaoh Amasis until the day when Cambyses became ruler of Egypt. He died on a mat(?) before he reached his country. Darius became king, whom (the rulers?) of the entire earth obeyed because of the excellence of his heart. He wrote to his satrap in Egypt (*Aryandes*) in year 3, saying thus: 'May the wise men be brought to me [...] among the warriors, the priests, and the scribes of Egypt [...] together (?), so that they write down the law of Egypt up to year 44 of the Pharaoh Amasis.'

The law [of the Pharaoh], the temples and the people was brought here [...] a papyrus up to year 19 [...] Egypt. They were [...] in year 27. They wrote a copy on papyrus, one in Assyrian script and one in documentary script (*Demotic*). It was completed in his presence. They wrote it in his presence; nothing was omitted.'

BN 215; Spiegelberg 1914, Devauchelle 1995

Several Demotic texts, written on the *verso* of a papyrus document, record Cambyses' policy towards the Egyptian temples (see above **24**), and provide an insight into Darius' policy in Egypt. The favourable comments which he seems to have attracted contrast with those made about Cambyses, and this may have been in consequence of a deliberate policy of Darius. But in principle he did exactly the same as his predecessors did, that is, appease the population by leaving as much as possible of their cultural and religious traditions unaltered.

Note that the original text was copied down in both Babylonian and Demotic.

Darius and Greece

When some of the Greek cities of Ionia revolted in 499 under the leadership of the tyrant Aristagoras of Miletus, the cities of Athens and Eretria sent only limited support consisting of twenty-five ships. Sardis was attacked and burned, but the ships returned without engaging the Persian fleet in battle. The Ionian Revolt took six years to quash. However, from a Persian perspective the revolt seems to have been regarded as a minor military problem, since Darius did not lead the campaign himself. The king's personal engagement in the campaign would signal the gravity of the conflict, as is attested for Assyrian and Babylonian kings in Near Eastern history. After the situation in Ionia had been resolved, Darius ordered a campaign to be mounted against the two Greek cities, Athens and Eretria, which had shown their support for the Ionian cities. This campaign, too, launched in 490, was under the command of Persian generals, Datis and Artaphernes, rather than of Darius himself. The size of the army sent to Greece emphasises that this campaign cannot be regarded as a Persian endeavour to conquer Greece. Darius' main reason for ordering a punitive campaign against Athens and Eretria was to establish Persian control over the Aegean Sea. The appearance of Athenian and Eretrian warships in the eastern Aegean posed a potential threat to that control, and Darius' aim was to demonstrate Persian power in this region. His order to send messengers to Greek cities to demand the offering of earth and water, the symbolic tokens by which a city or a people showed their recognition of the authority of the Persian king, was undertaken to signal Darius' intention to focus the campaign on these two cities.

No account of the Ionian Revolt or the campaign of 490 has survived in the Persian records, which obliges us to rely on biased Greek sources. One small glimpse of Persian activity can be gathered from a travel text documenting the journey of Datiya from Sardis back to the king in 494.

56 Datiya received 70 quarts of beer as rations. He carried a sealed document (Elam. *halmi*) of the king. He went forth from Sardis (via) express (service), (he) went to the king at Persepolis. Month 11, year 27. (At) Hidali.

PF-NN 1809; Lewis 1980

The Datiya mentioned in this text is marked out as a very high personage by the size of his beer ration and may be Datis, called the Mede, who was a commander in 490 (Hdt.6.94.2). Datis carries an authorisation to travel from the king, which means that he had begun his journey in Persepolis and was now returning from Sardis, receiving his rations for the day at Hidali, a village located along the Royal Road which leads to the Persian royal capital. The text, dated January/February 494, documents that Datis had travelled to Sardis at the time of the Revolt, possibly on a tour of inspection and co-ordination before the final campaign against the Ionians.

57 [43.4] With a vast number of ships and a large army assembled there, they *(the Persians)* crossed the Hellespont on their ships, and began to march through Europe, towards Eretria and Athens. [44.1] This was the pretext of their expedition; but it was also their intention to subdue as many of the Greek cities as possible; first their fleet subdued the Thasians, who did not even raise a hand against them, and then the infantry added the Macedonians to the subjects they already had. All the tribes nearer to them than the Macedonians had already been made subjects.

Herodotus 6.43.4–44.1

58 [48.1] After this, Darius wanted to know whether the Greeks intended to resist or submit. He therefore sent heralds in different directions throughout Greece with orders to demand earth and water for the king. [48.2] These were sent to Greece, while others messengers were sent to the cities on the sea-coast which paid him tribute, commanding that warships and transport vessels for horses be built. [49.1] So the cities set about these preparations; and the messengers who had gone to Greece received what the king's proclamation demanded from many of those who lived on the mainland and from all the islanders to whom they came with the demand. Among the islanders who agreed to give earth and water to Darius were the people of Aegina.

Herodotus 6.48.1–49.1

59 [94.1] While Athens was at war with Aegina, the Persian (king) was making his plans; a servant was always reminding him to remember the Athenians, and the Pisistratidae were always on hand to malign the Athenians; moreover, Darius wanted to use this as a pretext to subjugate those Greeks who had not offered him earth and water. [94.2] As for Mardonius, who had fared so ill with his armament, he dismissed him from his command, and appointed other generals to lead his armies against Athens and Eretria, Datis the Mede and his own nephew Artaphernes son of Artaphernes; and the charge he gave them on their departure was to enslave Athens and Eretria and to bring the slaves into his presence.

Herodotus 6.94

60 [59.4] After three more years as tyrant of Athens, Hippias was deposed by the Spartans and the exiled Alcmeonids in the fourth year *(510)*, and left under safe conduct for Sigeum and then went to Aeantides (*his son-in-law*) in Lampsacus, and from there to the court of Darius; from there he accompanied the Medes to Marathon twenty years later, being now an old man.

Thucydides 6.59.4

The Pisistratidae (**59**) were Hippias, the son and successor of the Athenian tyrant Pisistratus, and his sons. Hippias, who was driven out in 510 (**60**), fled to Persia and twenty years later advised the Persian commanders to land at Marathon. Among the Greek states which supported Persia were Thasos and Aegina, as well as Macedon. These states had offered earth and water to the king, thereby officially acknowledging his supremacy (see below p.53).

2.2. XERXES I
Seal and inscription of Xerxes from Dascylium
61   I am Xerxes, the King.

SXf; Schmitt 1981

9. Impression of Xerxes' seal from Dascylium

Impressions of Xerxes' seal were found on *bullae* from Dascylium, the satrapal centre of Phrygia in north-west Asia Minor. *Bullae* are lumps of clay which were attached to documents written on parchment or papyrus. They bear the seal impressions of high officials of the Persian administration. The above seal shows the king in the royal Persian dress, crowned and holding by its horns a winged beast standing upright; in his right hand the king holds a dagger. Behind the king stands a palm tree. The inscription is written in Old Persian only. The name Xerxes (OP *Xšayaršа*, Elam. *Ikšerišša*) means 'Ruling hero'.

Seal and inscription of Xerxes from Egypt

62   I am Xerxes.

SXe; Schmitt 1981

10. Impression of Xerxes' seal from Egypt

The cylinder seal is made of lapis lazuli and is 2.7 cm high. The seal, which was rather crudely cut, shows the king wearing a crown and holding a ring in his left hand while standing in front of a stylised tree. The inscription is written in Old Persian only.

Inscription from Persepolis

63   §1. Ahura Mazda is a great god, who created this earth, who created that sky, who created man, who created happiness for man, who made Xerxes king, one king of many, one lord of many.

§2. I am Xerxes, the Great King, king of kings, king of lands containing many men, king of this great earth far and wide, son of Darius the king, an Achaemenid.

§3. Xerxes the king says: 'By the favour of Ahura Mazda, I built this Gate of All Lands. Much other good (construction) was built within this (city of) Parsa, which I built and which my father built. Whatever good construction is seen, we built all that by the grace of Ahura Mazda.'

§4. Xerxes the king says: 'May Ahura Mazda protect me and my kingdom and what was built by me, and what was built by my father, that also may Ahura Mazda protect.'

XPa

The trilingual inscription is written in four copies on the inner walls of the Gate of All Lands, or Gate of All Nations, on the royal terrace in Persepolis. Xerxes' inscriptions follow the formula known from the inscriptions of Darius I. Xerxes presents himself in every respect as the successor of Darius, continuing his building work on the terrace of Persepolis, and following his father in tone and sentiments in the royal inscriptions. This continuity creates an image of kingship in which the preservation of a tradition established by Darius outweighs the need for individual expression. This adherence to the image of kingship persists throughout Achaemenid rule.

Inscription from Lake Van

64 §1. Ahura Mazda is a great god, who is the greatest of the gods, who created this earth, who created that sky, who created man, who created happiness for man, who made Xerxes king, one king of many, one ruler of many.
§2. I am Xerxes, the Great King, king of kings, king of (the) lands of many people, king of this great earth far and wide, son of Darius the king, the Achaemenid.
§3. Xerxes the king says: 'King Darius, who was my father, built much that is good, by the favour of Ahura Mazda. And he gave orders to carve out this niche, but he did not succeed in getting an inscription written (on it). Afterwards I ordered an inscription to be carved (on it). May Ahura Mazda as well as the other gods, protect me and my kingship and what I have built.'

XV

The trilingual inscription was written in a rectangular niche high on a precipitous rocky wall of the castle at Lake Van in northwest Iran. Inscriptions like this one were probably set up across the empire at places of historical significance for the Persian kings, on stone as well as on other materials which may not have survived.

Inscription from Mount Elvand

65 §1. Ahura Mazda is a great god, who is the greatest of the gods, who created this earth, who created that sky, who created man, who created happiness for man, who made Xerxes king, one king of many, one lord of many.
§2. I am Xerxes, the Great King, king of kings, king of (the) lands of many peoples, king of this great earth far and wide, son of Darius the king, the Achaemenid.

XE

See **47**.

Babylonian document for Belšimanni

66 [Murašu the scribe] spoke thus on day 1 of the month Ululu, accession year of [Belšimanni king of Babylon, before Nabu-aplu-iddina] the chief administrator of E-imbi-Anu (and) Nidintu-[...] the resident of (the temple) E-imbi-Anu to Nabu-ahu-ittannu the scribe: 'Why are you not performing the task of the scribe (any more)?' Nabu-ahu-ittannu spoke as follows: '[...] the work is done with, I will not undertake scribal work (any more).'
Then Nabu-ahu-ittannu and Murašu listened to one another, and as from day 1 of the month Ululu, accession year of Belšimanni king of Babylon, the writing board of the incoming payments, all of it, is allocated to Murašu, the scribe, son of Bel-iddina son of the Dabibi family, and the writing board of expenditure, all of it, is allocated to Nabu-ahu-ittannu, the scribe, son of Uraš-kasir the son of the Dabibi family. The income and expenditure from the month Addarru of the first year to the end of the month Abu, those of Murašu [...] those of Nabu-ahu-ittannu [...] their work of [...] of Nabu-bullissu and his colleagues [...] and his colleagues [...].
(...)

[Dilbat], day 1 of the month Ululu accession year of [Belšimanni] king of Babylon. Each party has taken a copy (of the document).

VS VI 331 (transl. H. Baker)

Some Babylonian documents dated to August 482/1 name Belšimanni as the king of Babylon, bearing either the title 'king of Babylon' or 'king of Babylon, king of lands'. He seems to have remained on the throne for only about a fortnight, but his attempt to make himself king will have forced Xerxes to act immediately, before embarking on his expedition to Greece. In the absence of any historical account of the events taking place in the Persian empire, evidence such as this economic text provides a small but crucial element in our understanding of the complexities of Xerxes' reign.

The Median War

67   [6.2] It so happened that messengers came from the Aleuadae (*the royal family*) in Thessaly, who invited the king into Greece with all their support. Furthermore, the Pisistratidae, who had come to Susa, did likewise, using the same arguments as the Aleuadae, and in addition urging him (*Xerxes*) even more strongly.

Herodotus 7.6.2

68   [14.2] It was only shortly before the Median War and the death of Darius (*I*) who succeeded Cambyses (*II*), that the tyrants of Sicily and the Corcyraeans acquired triremes on any scale; and these were the last navies worth mentioning in Hellas before the expedition of Xerxes. [14.3] The Aeginetans and Athenians and some others may have possessed a few vessels, but they were mostly *pentekontors*; it was only recently, when the Athenians were fighting the Aeginetans and also expecting the barbarian invasion, that Themistocles persuaded them to build the ships with which they fought in the sea-battle (*of Salamis*); and even these ships still did not have complete decks.

Thucydides 1.14.2–3

69   [23.1] The greatest achievement of the past was the Median War, and yet it was soon decided in two naval battles and two battles on land. In contrast, the Peloponnesian War was fought over a long period of time, and while it lasted, misfortunes befell Greece that were unmatched in any equal period of time.

Thucydides 1.23.1

The Greek expedition of Xerxes, undertaken in 480/79, is known in Greek historical texts as the 'Median War'. The Greeks used the terms 'Median' and Persian' without making any distinction between them. 'The Mede' was commonly used to refer to Persians. It is not certain whether the Greeks knew that the Medes and the Persians were different Iranian peoples.

With the expedition of 480/79 Xerxes carried out Darius' plans of a war against Greece after the campaign of 490, which had ended in the Persian withdrawal after Marathon. But Darius died in December 486, and before Xerxes could muster an army for his Greek expedition, he had to deal with a revolt in Egypt and possibly one in Babylonia. The period of ten years between 490 and 480 is often regarded as a time in which Greece as a whole foresaw the war with Persia and accordingly made preparations for it. However, Athens' main concern at that time was the war with Aegina, and Themistocles' shipbuilding programme was ostensibly aimed at that war rather than a conflict with Persia. The fact that a number of Greek states and islands were prepared to offer earth and water to Xerxes demonstrates that the Greeks were not united in a common ambition to fight the Persians. Thebes and Argos, like Thessaly, did not participate in the Median War, a fact that was held against them when it was over (Plut.*Them*.20.3; see LACTOR 1, no.6).

Medising

70   [95.3] In the meantime the Spartans recalled Pausanias in order to question him about various reports they were hearing; for he was charged with much injustice by the Greeks who arrived there, and gave the impression of a would-be tyrant rather than of a general. [95.4] And it happened that he was recalled at just the time when, out of their hatred for him, the allies, apart from the Peloponnesian force, had lined up with the Athenians. [95.5] Returning to Sparta, and condemned for various acts of injustice against individuals, he was acquitted of the main charges of misconduct and declared not guilty; he had been accused above all of medising, and the evidence had seemed very clear.

Thucydides 1.95.3–5

71   [135.2] Concerning the medism of Pausanias, the Spartans sent envoys to the Athenians and accused Themistocles of being implicated in the same crime as Pausanias, relying on the evidence they had discovered about him, and they demanded that he be punished in the same way. [135.3] The Athenians agreed to do so, but as he had already been ostracised and was living in Argos, from where he used to visit other parts of the Peloponnese, they sent some men, accompanied by Spartans who were prepared to join in the pursuit, with orders to arrest him wherever they found him.

Thucydides 1.135.2–3

72   [21.4] It is said that Timocreon was exiled because of his medising and that Themistocles was one of those who voted against him. [21.5] Therefore, when Themistocles himself was accused of medising, Timocreon wrote the following lines against him:

Timocreon is not alone

in having dealt with the Medes;

No, there are other vicious creatures too;

I'm not the only fox with a short tail:

there are others too.

Plutarch, *Themistocles* 21.4-5

After the Median War, the term 'medising' was used by the Greeks to accuse an individual or a state of conspiring with 'the Mede', meaning Persia. The accusations against the Spartan commander Pausanias and Themistocles are the best known ones (see LACTOR 1, nos.7–10). Timocreon was a Rhodian poet.

Greek evidence for the death of Xerxes

73   Artabanus, a powerful man close to Xerxes, together with Aspamithres, a eunuch, plotted to assassinate Xerxes; having assassinated him, they made his son Artaxerxes believe that it was Darius, his second son, who had killed him. Brought by Artabanus, Darius comes to the palace of Artaxerxes; with much shouting, he protests that he did not kill his father, but he is put to death.

Ctesias *FGrH* 688 F 13

74   Xerxes was killed by Artabanus because he was afraid of the rumours about (*Xerxes' son*) Darius, whom he had hanged against the orders of the king, hoping that the king would forget about it over his meal and be lenient.

Aristotle, *Politics* 1311b37–40

75   [69.1] During this year (*465*), in Asia Artabanus, a Hyrcanian by birth, who enjoyed the greatest influence at the court of king Xerxes, and was captain of the

royal bodyguard, decided to kill Xerxes and transfer the kingship to himself. (...)
[69.2] And Artabanus, being led at night by him (*Mithridates*) to his bedroom,
killed Xerxes and then went after the king's sons.

Diodorus Siculus 11.69.1–2

Xerxes was killed by the captain of his bodyguard, Artabanus, apparently in an attempt to overthrow the
Achaemenid dynasty and claim the throne for himself. Xerxes had ruled for twenty-one years as king of Persia.
Artabanus' coup, however, failed, and Xerxes' son Artaxerxes I succeeded to the throne (see also below **81**)

2.3. ARTAXERXES I
Inscription from Persepolis

76 §1. Ahura Mazda is a great god, who created this earth, who created that sky,
who created man, who created happiness for man, who made Artaxerxes king,
one king of many, one lord among many.

§2. I am Artaxerxes, the Great King, king of kings, king of lands, king of this
great earth far and wide, son of Xerxes the king, grandson of Darius the king, an
Achaemenid.

§3. Artaxerxes, the Great King, says: 'By the grace of Ahura Mazda I (continued to) build this palace, which my father king Xerxes (had begun to) build. May
Ahura Mazda protect me and my reign and what I have built.'

A^1 Pa

The bilingual text is inscribed on a marble block found in the courtyard before the south front of the throne-
hall of Artaxerxes I at Persepolis. Like Xerxes and Darius I before him, he continued the building programme
on the royal terrace. In this inscription Artaxerxes records the completion of the so-called 'One-Hundred-
Column-Hall', which was begun under Xerxes. The inscription shows that Artaxerxes I was firmly established in the Achaemenid dynasty, using Old Persian as the dynastic script in the royal trilingual inscriptions, following the wording of his predecessors. The name Artaxerxes (OP *Artaxšaça*, Elam. *Irdašašša*)
means 'He who reigns through truth'.

Inscription of Artaxerxes I on a silver dish

77 Artaxerxes, the Great King, king of kings, king of lands, son of Xerxes the king,
of Xerxes son of Darius the king, in whose royal house this silver dish was made.

A^{1}I

The Old Persian inscription is found on four silver dishes from an unknown provenance, now in the
Archaeological Museum in Tehran. Luxury items made of precious metals, like the silver dish, were commis-
sioned by the king himself and were sometimes presented as gifts to loyal subjects.

Vase Inscription of Artaxerxes

78 Artaxerxes, the Great Pharaoh.

A^{1}Orsk; Mayrhofer 1978

The inscription is written in Egyptian hieroglyphs on an alabaster vase, though fragments of the text in the
three standard cuneiform scripts can also be deciphered. The vase came originally from Egypt, but was found
in 1971 during building work carried out in Orsk, east of Orenburg, in southern Russia. Dated stylistically
to the reign of Artaxerxes I, the inscription acknowledges Artaxerxes as king of Egypt. The find-spot raises
the question of the distribution and recognition of Achaemenid royal art beyond the borders of the empire.

Documents from Egypt

79 Min of Koptos, Lord of the chapel Sehent. In the 5th year of the Lord of Upper
and Lower Egypt (*461/0*), Artaxerxes, who will live forever, loved by the gods.
Made by the Persian Ariyawrata, son of Arsames, born of the lady Qandjou, who
bows before Min, Horus, and Isis of Koptos.

Posener 1936: no.31

80   (Horus) the Great, son of Isis.

Year 16 of the Good God, Lord of the Two Lands, and year 17 (*450/49*), Artaxerxes, given eternal life, like Re.

May Min, Horus, and Isis of Koptos, and Amonrasonter, lord of the sky, grant life to the Persian Ariyawrata, called Djeho, son of Arsames, born of the lady Qandjou, who dwells before (Min, Horus, and Isis of Koptos, and Amonrasonter, lord of the sky).

Posener 1936: no.33

These dedications were written in hieroglyphic script on altars to honour the Egyptian gods worshipped in Koptos. The principal cults of Min, the Egyptian god of fertility, were located at Akhim and Koptos in Upper Egypt. The god was represented as ithyphallic, wearing a close-fitting garment. For Horus, see on **22**.

These dedications attest the presence of the Persian official Ariyawrata in Egypt. Ariyawrata was the son of Arsames and a woman called Qandjou, which is an Egyptian name. Like his brother Atiyawahy, Ariyawrata was a high official in Egypt (see below **131–132**). The first dedication was set up in 461/0, at the time of the revolt of Inaros in Egypt (see **84–88**). Artaxerxes' continued acceptance as king of Egypt in these dedications implies that the revolt did not affect the whole of Egypt, but was limited to the Delta region (see LACTOR 1, no.39).

Greek evidence for the reign of Artaxerxes
Accession of Artaxerxes

81   [69.2] Artabanus, being led at night by him (*Mithridates*) to his bedroom, killed Xerxes and then went after the king's sons. There were three of them, Darius the oldest and Artaxerxes, who were both living in the palace, and the third, Hystaspes, who was away at the time because he was governing the satrapy of Bactria. [69.3] Now Artabanus, approaching Artaxerxes while it was still dark, told him that his brother Darius had murdered his father and was transferring the kingship to himself. [69.4] He therefore advised him to ensure that he did not become a slave through inaction but punished his brother for his father's murder and became king himself, before Darius could seize the throne; he promised to secure him the co-operation of the king's bodyguard. [69.5] Artaxerxes took his advice and immediately, together with the help of the bodyguard, killed his brother Darius; when he (*Artabanus*) saw that he was succeeding with his plans, he summoned his own sons and said that now the time had come to seize the throne and struck Artaxerxes with his sword. [69.6] Being wounded but not badly hurt by the blow, he (*Artaxerxes*) held off Artabanus and dealing him a mortal blow, killed him. Thus Artaxerxes, after being saved in this unexpected fashion, and having avenged the murder of his father, succeeded to the Persian throne.

Diodorus Siculus 11.69.2–6

Artaxerxes succeeded to the Achaemenid throne in December 465, following an attempted coup by Artabanus (see above **73–75**). Artabanus had planned to murder not only Xerxes but also the king's sons, Darius, the designated heir to the throne, and Artaxerxes, who were in the palace at the time. Having been deceived into believing that his brother Darius had killed Xerxes, Artaxerxes in turn killed his brother, only to find himself threatened by Artabanus. By killing Artabanus Artaxerxes escaped death and succeeded to the Achaemenid throne.

Themistocles' refuge in Persia

82   [138.5] There is a monument to him in the central square of Asiatic Magnesia, where he was governor. The king (*Artaxerxes I*) gave him for bread Magnesia, which brought in a revenue of fifty talents a year, for wine, Lampsacus, reputed to have been the biggest wine-producer of all at that time, and Myus for fish.

Thucydides 1.138.5

Themistocles is one of several Greeks who sought refuge with the Persian king. When Hippias was forced to leave Athens in 510, he went eventually to the court of Darius I (Hdt.5.64-65; Thuc.6.59; see above **60**). Both Gongylos of Eretria and the Spartan king Demaratus found refuge in the Persian empire and were rewarded with cities (Xen. *Hell*. 3.1.6). Themistocles had fallen out of favour with the Athenians and was ostracised in his absence in about 469 (**71**). He reached Persia late in 465 (see also LACTOR 1: nos.35–36).

Revolts in Bactria and Egypt

83 Bactria, with its satrap, another Artabanus, revolted from Artaxerxes. A battle was fought but proved indecisive, and another battle was fought. And the wind blows against the Bactrians. Artaxerxes wins the victory, and all of Bactria surrenders.

Ctesias *FGrH* 688 F14

Following his accession to the throne, Artaxerxes had to deal with two revolts, one in Bactria, the other in Egypt. No precise dates for the revolt in Bactria are known, but Ctesias names an Artabanus as the satrap of Bactria and the leader of the revolt. In 500/499, a man called Irtabanuš is mentioned as satrap of Bactria in a text from Persepolis (PF 1287); it is possible that he was an ancestor of the Artabanus mentioned in this passage. But, according to Diodorus, the satrap of Bactria at that time was the second son of Xerxes, called Hystaspes (Diodorus Siculus 11.69.2; see above **81**).

84 [12.4] I saw similar skulls at Papremis (*Letopolis*), which once belonged to the men serving under Achaemenes son of Darius (I), who were destroyed by Inaros, the Libyan.

Herodotus 3.12.4

Achaemenes, the son of Darius I, led the Persian forces sent to quash the revolt of Inaros, but his army suffered defeat and heavy losses at Letopolis (**50**), and he himself was killed, *c*.459. Achaemenes was in fact the satrap of Egypt (Hdt.7.7). He was succeeded by Arsames, the grandson or great-grandson of Darius I (**184**), who was to remain in office for half a century.

85 [160.1] It is often said that Darius declared that he would rather have had Zopyrus unmutilated than twenty more Babylons. [160.2] He held him in great honour: every year he gave him such gifts as the Persians consider most precious, and for the rest of his life made him governor of Babylon, free from tax, and gave him much else too. This Zopyrus was the father of Megabyxus, who campaigned in Egypt against the Athenians and their allies; the son of Megabyxus was Zopyrus who deserted from the Persians to Athens.

Herodotus 3.160

In his second attempt to quash the revolt of Inaros (**84**), Artaxerxes I sent an army and a Persian fleet under the command of Megabyxus (2) and Artabazus. Megabyxus (2) was the son of Zopyrus (1) and the grandson of Megabyxus (1), who was one of the Persian nobles involved in overthrowing Bardiya/Gaumata (see DB IV: §68, **44**). Zopyrus (1) had proved himself devoted to Darius in 521, when he quashed a revolt in Babylon. The king rewarded him with gifts and special honours for the rest of his life (see also below **121- 122**) His son Megabyxus (2) proved himself hardly less devoted to Artaxerxes when he quashed the Egyptian revolt. He succeeded in driving the Greeks out of Memphis, and then his forces surrounded the Greeks and Egyptians on the island of Prosopitis. The Athenian fleet was defeated in 455/4 and forced to surrender (**88**).

86 [104.1] Inaros, son of Psammetichus, a Libyan and king of the Libyans who live next to Egypt - setting off from Mareia, the city just south of Pharos - caused the greater part of Egypt to revolt from king Artaxerxes, and then, when he had made himself ruler, called in the Athenians.

Thucydides 1.104.1

When Inaros had enticed Egypt to revolt from Persia, he called upon the Athenian fleet for support. The Athenians diverted the 200 ships under the command of Cimon from Cyprus to Egypt. Contrary to

Thucydides' statement, only part of the Delta of the Nile was in the hands of the rebels, including the White Fort, part of the city of Memphis (see **88**).

87   [109.4] He (*Megabyxus*) marched by land and defeated the Egyptians and their allies in battle, drove the Greeks out of Memphis and finally shut them up on the island of Prosopitis, where he besieged them for a year and six months, until, by diverting the water into another course, he drained the canal and left the ships high and dry, making most of the island part of the mainland. Then he marched over on foot and took the island.

(...) [110.2] And the whole of Egypt came again under the king's rule, except for Amyrtaeus, the king of the marshes (...). [110.3] Inaros, the king of the Libyans who had caused the revolt in Egypt, was taken by treachery and impaled.

Thucydides 1.109.4-110.3

Thucydides provides some information about the Athenian disaster in Egypt, which cost Athens a substantial part of her fleet. The revolt of Inaros had lasted from *c*.464/3 to 454. Egypt remained under Persian control until 404, when it revolted for a second time and remained independent until 343, when it was reconquered by Artaxerxes III. (For Thucydides' full account see LACTOR 1, no.39.)

88   [71.1] Artaxerxes, king of Persia, who had just secured his throne, began by punishing those who had played a part in the murder of his father and then arranged the affairs of the kingdom to suit himself. [71.2] As for the *hyparchoi* who were in office as satraps, he dismissed those who were hostile towards him, but from his friends he selected those who also were competent and gave them the satrapies. He also concerned himself with the revenues and the preparation of armaments, and as his rule was generally mild, he was held in great regard by the Persians. [71.3] But when the Egyptians learned of the death of Xerxes and the whole succession struggle and the upheaval amongst the Persians, they decided to fight for their freedom. So they at once mustered an army and revolted from the Persians, and after expelling the Persians who collected the tribute from Egypt, they appointed as their king a man named Inaros. [71.4] At first he recruited soldiers from Egypt, but later also recruited mercenaries from other lands, building up a strong army. He sent envoys to the Athenians to negotiate an alliance, promising them that, if they liberated the Egyptians, he would give them a share in the kingdom and present them with benefactions many times greater than the aid they had provided. [71.5] The Athenians considered it to their advantage to humble the Persians as much as they could, and to ally themselves with the Egyptians against ever-changing Fortune and voted to send three hundred warships to support the Egyptians. [71.6] With great enthusiasm the Athenians began to prepare for the expedition. Meanwhile Artaxerxes, on hearing about the revolt of the Egyptians and their preparations for war, decided that his forces must outnumber those of the Egyptians. So at once he began to recruit soldiers from all the satrapies, to build ships and to concern himself with every other aspect of the preparations. (...)

[74.1] Artaxerxes, king of Persia, appointed Achaemenes, the son of Darius and his own uncle, as commander against the Egyptians; he put him in charge of more than three hundred thousand soldiers, counting both cavalry and infantry; he commanded him to crush the Egyptians. [74.2] When he had arrived in Egypt, Achaemenes set up his camp near the Nile, and when he had rested his army after the march, he prepared for battle; the Egyptians, having gathered their army from

Libya and Egypt, were waiting for their Athenian allies. [74.3] When the Athenians had arrived in Egypt with two hundred ships and had drawn up with the Egyptians opposite the Persians, a mighty battle ensued. For some time the Persians with their superior numbers prevailed, but then, when the Athenians took the offensive, routing the forces opposing them and killing many of them, the rest of the barbarians took flight. [74.4] There was much slaughter in the course of the flight, and finally the Persians, having lost most of their army, escaped to the White Fort (*part of Memphis*). The Athenians, who had owed their victory to their own valour, pursued the barbarians to the above mentioned place and did not fail to besiege it. [74.5] Artaxerxes, hearing of the defeat of his troops, first sent some of his friends with vast amounts of money to Sparta to ask the Spartans to invade Attica, thinking that in that case the Athenians who had been victorious in Egypt would sail back to Athens to defend their city; [74.6] however, the Spartans neither accepted the money nor listened to the requests of the Persians, and Artaxerxes despaired of getting aid from the Spartans. He therefore began preparing fresh forces; he put Artabazus and Megabyxus in command, men of high distinction, and sent them to make war on the Egyptians. (...)

[75.2] When they arrived in Cilicia and Phoenicia, they rested their land forces after the journey and ordered the Cyprians and Phoenicians and Cilicians to supply ships. When three hundred triremes had been prepared, they equipped them with the best marines, and arms and missiles, and everything else that is needed in a naval battle. [75.3] So the commanders (*Artabazus and Megabyxus*) were occupied with their preparations and the training of the soldiers, familiarising all with the facts of warfare, and they spent almost the whole year like this. [75.4] Meanwhile in Egypt the Athenians were still besieging those who had escaped to the White Fort in Memphis, but because the Persians were defending themselves well, they were unable to take the fort, and thus spent the year on the siege. (...)

[77.1] In Asia, the Persian commanders who had moved on to Cilicia prepared the three hundred ships which they fully equipped for war, and then they marched with their soldiers through Syria and Phoenicia; accompanied by the fleet sailing along the coast, they reached Memphis in Egypt. [77.2] First of all they broke the siege of the White Fort, having terrified the Egyptians and the Athenians; then, adopting a prudent strategy, they avoided any direct attack and were eager to end the war through the use of stratagems. Thus, since the Athenian ships were anchored off the island called Prosopitis, they diverted the river which flowed around the island by digging canals, making the island part of the mainland. [77.3] When the ships were suddenly stranded, the Egyptians, in fear, deserted the Athenians and came to terms with the Persians; the Athenians, left without an ally, and seeing that their ships had become useless, burnt them in order to prevent them falling into the hands of their enemy, and then, undismayed at this alarming plight, fell to exhorting one another to do nothing unworthy of the battles they had won in the past. [77.4] Thus, showing valour surpassing that of those who died at Thermopylae in defence of Greece, they were ready to face the enemy in battle. But the generals Artabazus and Megabyxus, recognising the outstanding courage of their enemies, and reasoning that they would be unable to destroy these men without the sacrifice of many myriads of their own men, made a truce with the Athenians under which they should leave Egypt in safety. [77.5] Thus, the Athenians, having saved their lives by their valour, left Egypt and went via Libya to Cyrene and most surprisingly returned safely to their homeland.

Diodorus Siculus 11.71–77

Diodorus dates the outbreak of the revolt in Egypt shortly after the accession of Artaxerxes I, in 464/3. Having failed to secure the political and military support of Sparta, the Persian forces first attacked the rebels under the command of Achaemenes, but were defeated and had to retreat. A second force under Artabazus and Megabyxus managed to isolate the Athenians and force them to surrender, thereby ending the revolt in 454. Diodorus endorses Artaxerxes' policy of ensuring immediately after his accession to the throne the loyalty of his satraps. Greek writers sometimes use the term *hyparchos* instead of satrap (38).

The Peace of Callias of 449/8

The evidence for the Peace of Callias comes from Greek sources. The peace, which may have been concluded in 449/8, was preceded by several Greek embassies to Susa. The evidence for the Greek negotiations with Persia is discussed in full in LACTOR 1, nos. 50-63. The two passages quoted below provide only a brief note on this important development.

89   [151] It chanced that while Athenian envoys, Callias son of Hipponicus and the rest who had come up with him, were at Susa, called the city of Memnon, about some other business, the Argives also had at the same time sent envoys to Susa to ask Artaxerxes, the son of Xerxes, whether the bond of friendship which they had formed with Xerxes was still valid, or whether he considered them his enemies.

Herodotus 7.151

An Athenian embassy under Callias was sent to Susa to confirm the *status quo* between Athens and Persia. It is not possible to date the above Athenian embassy other than through relative chronology: the passage reveals that the Athenian delegation stayed at Susa at the same time as envoys from Argos. However, the presence of another embassy may indicate that this event occurred shortly after the accession of Artaxerxes I in 465, as this would have been the time to confirm agreements made with the previous king. To what extent Callias' mission was undertaken with a permanent treaty in mind is impossible to say.

90   [4.5] Those with Artabazus and Megabyxus sent ambassadors (*in 449*) to Athens to discuss a settlement. The Athenians reacted favourably and dispatched ambassadors with full powers, under the leadership of Callias son of Hipponicus. And so the Athenians and their allies concluded with the Persians a treaty of peace, whose principal terms were: All the Greek cities of Asia are autonomous, the satraps of the Persians are not to come closer to the sea than a three-day journey, and no Persian warship is to sail inside (*west*) of Phaselis (*in Lycia*) or the Cyanean Rocks (*at Byzantium, the entrance to the Black Sea*). And if these terms are observed by the king and his generals, the Athenians are not to send troops into the territory over which the king is ruler.

Diodorus Siculus 12.4.5

Diodorus records the terms of the treaty between Persia and Athens, negotiated by Callias and other Athenians. Under these terms both Athenian activities in Asia Minor and Persian activity in the Aegean are restricted so that neither side should pose a military threat to the other. In addition, Persia has to recognise the self-government of the Greek cities of Asia Minor.

The death of Artaxerxes

91   Hallili son of Aqabbi-ili, Riqat-ili, and Iltammeš-lintar son of Bel-ah-iddin said to Rimut-Ninurta son of Murašu: "Please give us 1 *kur* 2 (*pan*) 3 *sut* of millet, and we will give you 300 water birds, large and small."

Rimut-Ninurta heard them, and he will give them 1 *kur* 2 (*pan*) 3 *sut* of millet, and by the 15th of Nisannu they will give 300 water birds, large and small, in their entirety.

Witnesses: Belšunu son of Erība-Enlil, Bel-dannu son of Ahhe-eriba, Iqišaya son
of Šum-iddin [erasure]

Scribe: Taqš-Gula son of Iddin-Enlil.

Place: Hašba.

Date: 17th Šabatu, year 41 of Artaxerxes (I), king of lands.

BE IX 109 (transl. H. Baker)

One of the latest texts from Babylonia dated to the reign of Artaxerxes I, this Babylonian business document from Hašba (location unknown) is dated 26 February 423. However, the earliest Babylonian documents giving a date for Artaxerxes' successor Darius II (Ochus) were written in the Babylonian city of
Nippur on 24 February 423 (BE X 2 and 3). Possibly the news of Artaxerxes' death and the accession of the
new king was received after a short delay. From these texts it appears that the forty-first year of Artaxerxes'
reign was also counted in Babylonia as the accession year of Darius II. Darius II succeeded to the Achaemenid
throne between December 424 and February 423.

92   Amestris (*the wife of Xerxes*) dies in very old age and Artaxerxes dies, having
         reigned for forty-two years. (...) After the death of Artaxerxes, it is Xerxes, his
         son, who holds the kingship; he was the only son he had by Damaspia, who died
         on the same day as Artaxerxes. Bagorazos conducted the bodies of his father and
         mother back to Parsa (*Persepolis*).

Ctesias *FGrH* 688 F 15

93   Artaxerxes, king of Persia, died after a reign of forty years, and the kingship was
         passed to Xerxes (*II*), who ruled for one year.

Diodorus Siculus 12.64.1

Diodorus attests a forty-year reign for Artaxerxes, stating that he died in 425/4, but this date can be corrected
by the Babylonian evidence. Contrary to his statement, Artaxerxes' designated heir, his son Xerxes (II),
ruled for only 45 days before he was killed by his half-brother Sogdianus. The short reign explains why no
Babylonian documents are dated by reference to Xerxes II's reign. Sogdianus in turn was overthrown by
another half-brother, Ochus, having been in power for too brief a period of time to have economic documents dated to his reign. Ochus succeeded to the throne, taking the throne-name Darius II.

Part III. The Organisation and Administration of the Empire; Religion in the Empire

Note C Persian Imperial Government

At the centre of imperial rule stood the Persian king. Yet this is not to say that the Persian empire was totally centralised. On the contrary, wherever it was advantageous for the king to leave local rule in place, he did so, provided that the local ruler recognised the king's authority and expressed his loyalty to the king. The Persian empire was governed through a number of satrapies, headed by the satrap, who was appointed by the king. The satrap was a member of the Persian nobility, and often a relative of the king or a noble Persian who had married into the royal family. Satraps represented royal power in the administrative centre of a satrapy, where taxes in the form of precious metal, grain, and livestock, were collected and stored, and records were kept concerning the economic affairs and annual accounts of the satrapal administration. Treasury officials, administrators and accountants were employed as servants of the satraps, controlling the storehouses and administering satrapal affairs. If political circumstances required them to do so, satraps took the command of an army, mustered at satrapal level. Local rulers who governed city-states, like the Phoenician cities, or semi-independent kings, like the dynasts of Caria in the fourth century, probably managed their affairs in a similar way. The pastoralists of the Zagros mountains, and the Scythian tribes at the northern borders of the empire, enjoyed a semi-independent status and, their lifestyle not requiring a fixed administration, they probably lacked any form of written records. Yet although these peoples were not under the direct control of the Persian king, they were part of the Persian empire.

Around the king was a group of Persian nobles, acting as courtiers, advisors and high-ranking officials in the Persian administration. At the end of the sixth century the highest office at court was occupied by Parnaka, the uncle of Darius I, heading the administration of Persepolis and Persis. Every official within that administration was under the control of Parnaka, beginning with Zissawis, his second-in-command, his office scribes, followed by the officials who controlled the different storehouses, for grain, wine, fruit and cattle. Parnaka's written orders were dictated to a scribe, and the message was passed on to the official concerned. At the royal storehouses, any order was recorded, accounting for any amount of food leaving or entering the storehouse. Monthly and annual accounts were kept by official accountants, who inspected the storehouse records and collected their information in so-called account texts. In the same way, through tax-handlers, taxes were collected from individuals or collectively from places, and records accounting for the taxes were kept in the Persepolis archive. This very detailed way of record-keeping was used to account for food rations issued to the workers in Persis, but also included rations for the high officials and even foodstuffs used by members of the royal family themselves. Most illuminating are the travel texts, documenting journeys undertaken by individuals or groups of people, who, provided with an official document approving their travel, were entitled to draw rations from royal storehouses. The daily withdrawal of foodstuffs must mean that storehouses existed along the Royal Roads at a day's journey from one another, which allowed the traveller to collect his or her food and likewise fodder and water for the animals.

The Persian empire comprised a vast number of different peoples with different cultures and a large variety of languages. Each satrapy continued to use its own local language or languages, and their administration was continued in their own script, as can be seen in the case of the Babylonian documents. The Persians did not impose one dominant language on all the satrapies, but administered them on a multilingual basis. Thus, although Elamite is the administrative script used in the archives of Persepolis, Babylonian scribes are attested working in the same administration. The find of five hundred clay tablets written in Aramaic script in the Persepolis archive (still unpublished) shows that the use of different languages and scripts did not present a problem for the central administration. It has been thought, however, that Aramaic was the language and script most widely used within the empire, and possibly the one language which overrode others. It has even been suggested that it was used as a *lingua franca*, especially in the later stages of the empire, but this suggestion is partly based on the fact that no cuneiform tablets have been recovered dating later than the reign of Artaxerxes I. Without further archaeological evidence, it is hard to determine whether the lack of clay tablets in the later stages of the empire marks a deliberate change in the administration or is merely fortuitous.

3.1. PERSIAN KINGSHIP
Royal titulature

94 Cyrus (*I*) of Anshan, son of Teispes.

1

95 Cyrus (*II*), king of Anshan.

11:II.1

96 Cyrus (*II*), king of Parsu.

11:II.15

97 Cambyses (*II*), king of Babylon, king of lands.

18

98 Barziya, king of Babylon, king of lands.

41

99 I (am) Darius (*I*), the Great King, king of kings, king of (*lit. in*) Persia, king of lands, the son of Hystaspes, the grandson of Arsames, an Achaemenid.

44:I: §1

100 I am Darius, the Great King, king of kings, king of lands containing many men, king of this great earth far and wide, son of Hystaspes, an Achaemenid, a Persian, son of a Persian, an Aryan, having Aryan lineage.

46: §2

101 I am Xerxes, the Great King, king of kings, king of lands containing many men, king of this great earth far and wide, son of Darius the king, an Achaemenid.

63: §2

102 I am Artaxerxes (*I*), the Great King, king of kings, king of lands, king of this great earth far and wide, son of Xerxes the king, grandson of Darius the king, an Achaemenid.

76: §2

The early Persian kings from Cyrus I to Bardiya were kings of Anshan or kings of Parsu/Parsa. The first title is reminiscent of the royal title of the Elamite kings, who were kings of Anshan and Susa. Its adoption by the early Persian kings reflects their ambition to be regarded as successors to the kings of Elam. The title 'king of Parsu/Parsa' refers to the region of Persis in southern Iran, where Iranian peoples had settled, and from which grew first a Persian principality, and eventually the Persian empire. Following the conquest of Babylonia in 539, Babylonian documents refer to the Persian kings as 'king of Babylon, king of lands'. With the beginning of the reign of Darius I the king was regularly referred to as 'Great King' and 'king of kings'. The title, 'king of kings', was used in a historical sense, which means that the king saw himself as the last in the line of his royal predecessors. Such an understanding of kingship, embedded in a tradition of royal rule, reflects a high awareness of history, and the king's own role in it. The Achaemenid king was 'king of Persia', meaning Parsa/Persis, and 'king of lands', a reference to all the other countries which were ruled by the Persian king. The Achaemenid kings did not use the term 'empire', as the Romans did later on for their realm, but referred to the territory and its inhabitants over which they ruled as 'lands' or 'peoples' (OP *dahyāva* can be translated in either way). This is in accordance with their political attitude towards those lands, which aimed at leaving in place local customs and religion, and even forms of political rule and semi-autonomy, as long as the lands paid tribute to the king and were loyal to him. A 'Persianisation', matching the Romanisation known from the Roman imperial period, was neither intended nor desired.

The most detailed royal title also included the king's genealogy, in which the king first mentioned his family by referring to his father, then defined his clan (Achaemenid), his tribe (Persian), and his ethnic origin (Aryan). In the conquered lands of the Persian empire, the royal title still followed the traditional form. Thus, in Egypt, the Persian kings were regarded as pharaohs and bore the title 'king of Upper and Lower Egypt'.

The ideology of kingship
Second inscription from Naqš-e Rustam

103   §1. Ahura Mazda is a great god, who created this excellent work which is seen, who created happiness for man, who bestowed wisdom and courage upon Darius the king.

§2. Darius the king says: 'By the favour of Ahura Mazda I am of such a kind that I am a friend of the Right, and not a friend of the Wrong; it is not my desire that the weak man should suffer injustice at the hands of the strong, it is not my desire that the strong man should suffer injustice from the weak.

§3. I desire what is Right. I am not a friend of the man who follows the Lie. I am not hot-tempered; the things that develop in me during a dispute I hold firmly under control through my mind, I am firmly in control of myself.

§4. I reward the man who seeks to contribute according to his efforts; I punish him who does harm, according to the harm done; I do not wish that a man should do harm; nor do I wish that, if he should do harm, he should not be punished.

§5. What a man says against a man, does not convince me, until I hear the testimony of both.

§6. I am content with what a man does or brings (as tribute) (for me) according to his abilities, my pleasure is great, and I am well disposed towards him.

§7. Of such a kind is my understanding and my judgement: when you shall see or hear of what I have done in the palace and on the battle-field, this is the will power which I possess over my mind and my understanding.

§8. This indeed is my courage as far as my body possesses the strength; as a commander I am a good commander; immediately, the right decision is taken according to my understanding when I meet a rebel, and when I meet (someone who is) not a rebel, at this moment, due to my understanding and judgement, I know that I am above panic when I see a rebel as well as when I see (someone who is) not a rebel.

§9. I am trained in my hands and in my feet; as a horseman, I am a good horseman; as a bowman, I am a good bowman, both on foot and on horseback; as a spearman, I am a good spearman, both on foot and on horseback.

§10. These are the skills which Ahura Mazda has bestowed upon me, and which I have been strong enough to exercise. By the favour of Ahura Mazda, what I have done, I have achieved with the skills that Ahura Mazda has bestowed upon me.

§11. O man, proclaim loud and clear of what kind you are, and of what sort your abilities are, and of what kind your loyalty is. Let that which has been heard by your ears not seem false to you; hear that which has been said to you!

§12. O man, let that which I have done not seem to you to be false; observe what the weak man has done. O man, see what I have done [...] not to overstep [...] and do not be ill disposed towards happiness [...].

DNb; Lecoq 1997

The second inscription on the tomb façade of Darius' tomb at Naqš-e Rustam is a testament of Darius, as well as a charter of Achaemenid kingship. Darius describes the values which define Persian kingship, within the dualities of right and wrong, truth and falsehood, loyalty and rebellion. Thus he recognises the values of the Right, or the Truth, the moral values which determine the religion of Ahura Mazda. The king himself is the first man in his empire to act according to righteousness, truth and justice, because he reigns with the support of Ahura Mazda. The Persian king, though not a divine being himself, is a ruler through whom Ahura Mazda expresses divine values. Through Ahura Mazda, the king's deeds and decisions achieve moral weight, while at the same time the king is the first to be judged by these values.

Darius describes himself as a Persian, who is a good commander and horseman, a good bowman and spearman. He wants to be regarded as the first man in the empire, that is, the first to contribute those abilities which are valued highest in Persian social life, as they ensure the defence and preservation of the empire. The king as the 'model ruler' and the 'model Persian' are the two images that Darius wants to convey in his inscription. The values expressed here are echoed in Herodotus (**105**).

Darius' inscription from Persepolis

104 §1. Ahura Mazda (is) great, the greatest of gods. He created Darius the king, he bestowed the kingdom on him. By the favour of Ahura Mazda, Darius is king.

§2. Darius the king says: 'This country, Persia, which Ahura Mazda bestowed upon me, is good, and possesses good horses and possesses good soldiers. By the favour of Ahura Mazda, and of me, Darius the king, it does not feel fear of any other.'

§3. Darius the king says: 'May Ahura Mazda bring me aid, together with all the gods; and may Ahura Mazda protect this country from a (*hostile*) army, from famine, from the Lie! Upon this country may there not come an army, or famine, or the Lie. This I pray as a blessing from Ahura Mazda, together with all the gods. May Ahura Mazda together with the other gods grant me this blessing.'

DPd

The monolingual inscription written in Old Persian was set up on the outer south wall of the royal terrace of Persepolis. It was possibly one of the earliest inscriptions carved on the royal terrace.

The inscription establishes the Persian god Ahura Mazda as the principal god of the Achaemenid kings. The Persian king acts under his protection and with his support. His rule is guided by the moral values set by Ahura Mazda. His rule is not the wilful rule of a despot, but is defined by morally good deeds and truthfulness. The ideology of kingship finds its ideal expression in the combination of the supreme rule of the king and the protection of Ahura Mazda under which the king reigns. As guardian of the empire, it is the king's responsibility to protect everyone and everything that represents the values of that empire, the peoples and the horses. The peoples are the loyal subjects who form the basis of the pyramidal structure of Persian society. They ensure prosperity and peace for the empire by living peacefully with each other as well as by accepting their king. The reference to horses reflects their vital importance for Persian life (see **45** §2). Within the empire they facilitate communication between the king and his peoples, enabled through the royal roads and the extensive system of post-stations (see **181–183**). They assure the rapid transmission of news and information within the empire, allowing the king to act swiftly. Militarily, the cavalry, introduced by Cyrus II (Xen.*Cyr*.1.3.3), played a central role in the Persian army, ensuring the defence of the empire.

The king represents the moral principles of the empire, and he condemns everything which is contrary to morally good behaviour, such as disloyalty and lying. By the principles of Persian kingship, disloyalty would occur if anyone disobeyed the king or threatened his rule. Furthermore, Darius seeks protection from any external threat to society, such as the invasion of a foreign army or famine.

Darius wants to present an empire which exists at peace with itself and without external enemies. The people from all the lands of his empire are seen as loyal, law-abiding subjects, while their king's rule is just. The peacefulness of the empire is achieved by following the wishes of Ahura Mazda, 'who created happiness for man'. Thus Darius creates an image of the empire, within which all the different peoples live a peaceful existence, a '*pax Persica*', or Persian peace. The ideal of a Persian peace, which was echoed by Darius' successors, is expressed in the royal inscriptions as well as in Achaemenid royal art and architecture.

Darius invokes other (Iranian and non-Iranian) gods in this text. They are not further specified, and the names of the gods Darius is referring to are not known. The Persepolis Fortification texts mention Elamite and Babylonian gods to whom sacrifices were made by Persian priests. The reference to these gods gives special importance to the inscription (see also **192**).

Persian education

105   Next to prowess in arms the strongest proof of manly excellence (*amongst the Persians*) is fathering many sons; every year the king sends gifts to the man who can show the highest number of sons. In their eyes number is strength. They educate their boys from the age of five to the age of twenty, and teach them only three things, to ride, to use a bow and arrows and to tell the truth. Until he is five years old, a boy is not seen by his father, but he lives with the women. This is done in case the child dies young, so that his father does not suffer distress.

Herodotus 1.136

Herodotus echoes the moral values respected by the Persian king, as expressed in the royal inscriptions (**103** §9). The desire for multiple offspring likewise is attested in the Bisitun Inscription (**44**: §§60, 66).

106   The Athenian: [694c] Very well, I divine that Cyrus, who otherwise no doubt was a good general and patriotic, was quite unconcerned with the principles of education and paid no attention to household management.

        Clinias: How are we to take a remark like that? [694d]

        The Athenian: It is likely that from boyhood onwards he spent his life on campaign and made over his sons to be reared by women. They raised them from infancy, telling them how fortunate and blessed they already were, because they lacked no component of the conditions that made them happy; and because they forbade anybody to oppose them in anything, on the grounds that they were so happy, and compelled everyone to praise everything they said or did, they turned them into what they became.

        Clinias: A fine education indeed, to judge from your description! [694e]

        The Athenian: Rather say an effeminate education, provided by royal women who had recently become rich, and who brought up the sons in the absence of their menfolk, who were kept busy by wars and endless dangers.

        Clinias: That sounds reasonable.

The Athenian: But their father, while acquiring cattle, sheep, herds of men and flocks of animals of all kinds, and in great numbers for them, was not aware that those to whom he would leave all this, were not being instructed in traditional Persian practice, which, since the Persians were shepherds, products of a harsh country, was rough and capable of training sturdy shepherds who could live out in the open, keep awake on watch and go campaigning if need be. [695a] He failed to notice that his sons' education had been ruined by the pretence of a happy upbringing, a Median education, which the women and the eunuchs gave his sons, [695b] and so they turned out as you would expect after having experienced an education without restraint. When his sons took over the kingship after Cyrus' death, full of luxury and without discipline, first one killed the other, because he did not want to regard him as an equal, then he himself, being demented by drunkenness and indiscipline, lost his own empire to the Medes, and to a man called 'the Eunuch', who despised the folly of Cambyses. [695c]

Clinias: This is what is said, and I believe that it is close to the truth.

The Athenian: And what is more, it is said that Persian kingship was restored by Darius and the Seven.

Clinias: So it is.

The Athenian: Let us then continue the story. Darius was not a royal son, nor was he brought up in luxury; so when he came to take the kingship supported by six nobles he divided the empire into seven parts, of which small vestiges still exist today; he thought it right to rule through laws into which he himself introduced a measure of equality for all, [695d] and incorporated in his laws the tribute-payments which Cyrus had promised the Persians, thereby generating friendliness and fellow feeling among all the Persians and winning them over through generosity with money and gifts; consequently the army's devotion to him ensured that he added at least as much land as Cyrus had left. After Darius came Xerxes, brought up again on the indulgent royal model of education of the royal house: 'Darius', as we may rightly say to him, 'you have not learned from the misfortune which befell Cyrus, [695e] and you have educated Xerxes on the same lines as he did Cambyses.' Thus Xerxes, the product of the same upbringing, repeated the bad deeds of Cambyses; in short, since then there has been scarcely any other king of the Persians who was indeed 'Great', and not merely so named. The reason, according to my argument, does not lie in luck, but in the bad life which is usually lived by the sons of the very rich and of tyrants: [696a] it is impossible for these ever to emerge from such an education a boy or a man or an old man who excels in virtue. This, we affirm, a lawgiver must consider, as we must on this occasion.

Plato, *Laws* 694c–696a

The image of a decadent, weak and effeminate Persian empire is prevalent in fourth-century Greek historiography. The alleged cause of this effeminacy is the fact that the Persian king is educated by women and eunuchs. While Cyrus' strength was due to his humble upbringing, his son Cambyses was already the victim of the decadence of the court. Darius, whom Plato describes as non-royal, having been brought up outside the court, was spared such an education and therefore succeeded in gaining control of the empire. The notion expressed here is based on ideological views rather than historical facts. The idea of the decline of the Persian empire beginning with Cambyses, briefly interrupted by the strong reign of Darius I, stands in contrast with the fact that Cambyses conquered Egypt and some of Nubia, as well as the fact that after Darius I the Achaemenid dynasty reigned without any serious threat until the 330's.

Succession to the throne

107 Xerxes the king says: 'Other sons of Darius there were, (but) it was the desire of Ahura Mazda that my father Darius made me the greatest after himself. When my father Darius left the throne, by the will of Ahura Mazda I became king on my father's throne. When I became king, I built much excellent (construction). I protected what had been built by my father and I added other buildings. Moreover, what I built, and what my father built - we built all that by the favour of Ahura Mazda.'

XPf: §4

A Persian king chose the heir to the throne out of several sons born by royal wives, who were daughters of Persian nobles. Persian kings practised polygamy because each king needed to produce a number of male offspring (see above **44; 105**), from whom he eventually selected the designated heir. In the case of Darius' choice of Xerxes, the inscription explicitly states that Xerxes was selected from several royal sons. The expression used in the Old Persian text, 'the greatest after himself' (OP *maθišta*), describes Xerxes' position as crown prince. Xerxes himself was the son of Darius and Atossa, the daughter of Cyrus II (**108**).

The reference to new building work carried out by Xerxes, and to his preservation of buildings constructed by Darius I shows that official royal architecture was an expression of Persian kingship.

108 [2.2] Before he became king, Darius had three sons by his first wife, the daughter of Gobryas, and four by Atossa the daughter of Cyrus, after he had become king. Of the earlier sons Artobarzanes was the oldest, and of the later ones Xerxes. [2.3] As they were from different mothers, they were rivals, Artobarzanes claiming that he was the oldest of all the children and that it was the custom among all men that the oldest should rule, Xerxes, that he was the son of Atossa, the daughter of Cyrus, and that it had been Cyrus who had freed the Persians.

Herodotus 7.2.2–3

In order to be able to succeed to the Persian throne it was important that the heir to the throne was born when the king was already enthroned and that his mother came from a Persian noble family. In the case of Xerxes' succession the decisive factor for Darius must have been that Atossa was the daughter of Cyrus, and her sons could lay a legitimate claim to succeed to the throne, whereas Darius did not belong to the royal family.

Royal residences

109 [6.22] Cyrus (*II*) himself made his home in the centre of his domain, and in the winter season he spent seven months in Babylon, for there the climate is warm. In the spring he spent three months in Susa and at the height of the summer two months in Ecbatana. By doing so, it is said, he enjoyed the warmth and coolness of perpetual springtime.

Xenophon, *Cyropaedia*.8.6.22

The Persian empire had several royal capitals: Ecbatana, the former capital of the Median king, Susa, one of the two capitals of Elam, and Babylon, the capital city of Babylonia. Satrapal centres included Sardis in Lydia, Dascylium in Phrygia, Memphis in Egypt, Damascus in Syria, Kandahar in Arachosia, and Bactra in Bactria (modern Balkh). The Persian king moved around throughout the seasons to reside in one of the palaces of his royal cities. When moving between his royal cities, the king travelled with his entire entourage, the royal women, courtiers, attendants, and the royal bodyguards. The royal progress was a massive spectacle, which demonstrated the king's power in the empire.

As manifestation of his kingship, Cyrus II built his own royal residence at Pasargadae, and Darius I began the construction of a new royal city, Persepolis, which became the ultimate expression of Achaemenid kingship. The successors of Darius I all followed the architectural style he had created with Persepolis, adhering to a royal Achaemenid style, which placed their kingship in a historical context. It was an expression of Achaemenid kingship, in which each king saw himself as a part of a dynastic tradition, perpetuating almost eternal values, as opposed to an individual king who, without a tradition, needed to impress his own personal style.

Royal estates
Partetaš
110 75 olive seedlings, 241 *karukur* seedlings, 60 *kazla* seedlings, 5 *silti* seedlings, 384 apple seedlings, 30 quince seedlings, 70 mulberry seedlings, 303 pear seedlings, in total 1,168 tree seedlings for planting. At (the place) Pirdubatti, the *partetaš*. For Mišputra to keep.

1,800 *karukur* seedlings, 40 apple seedlings, 27 pear seedlings, a total of 1,867 tree seedlings for planting. At (the place) Pirdubatti, at the storehouse. For (the man) Wulla to keep.

Total 3,035 tree seedlings for planting. Accounted for at Pirdubatti. 552 apple seedlings, 442 pear seedlings, 59 quince seedlings, 196 *karukur* seedlings, in total 1,249 tree seedlings for planting. At Tikranuš, the *partetaš*. For Zimakka to keep.(...)

114 apple seedlings, 22 mulberry seedlings, 54 olive seedlings, (...) 274 *karukur* seedlings, 80 date seedlings, 57 pear seedlings. In total 697 tree seedlings for planting. At Appištapdan, the *partetaš*. For [...] to keep.(...)

PFa 33

In the Persepolis Fortification texts '*partetaš*' means a royal estate, but the term can also mean a royal garden or park. Here seedlings for trees for three different royal estates in Persis are recorded. Although not all Elamite words used here can be translated, it is clear from the context that these were all seedlings of fruit trees. The Elamite *partetaš* reflects an Old Persian word **pairi- daeza-*, which means 'walled space'; the word was translated into Greek as *paradeisos* and is first used by Xenophon.

A satrap complains
111 'My father left me (*Pharnabazus*) fine houses and parks, full of trees and wild animals, in which I took delight. Now they are either cut down or burnt down.'

Xenophon, *Hellenica* 4.1.33

Parks not only surrounded the residences of the Persian kings, but, as Greek sources confirm, were also enjoyed by satraps. Satraps copied the lifestyle of the Persian king on a local scale, as they represented the king in the satrapies. Xenophon records the destruction of the gardens of Pharnabazus, the satrap of Hellespontine Phrygia at Dascylium, by the Spartan commander Agesilaus.

High-ranking Persian noblemen
Gobryas and Aspathines
112 Gobryas, a Patischorian, the Spear-bearer of Darius the King.

DNc

Gobryas' prominent position among the Persian nobles is emphasised by his role as the king's Spear-bearer, who is depicted in the Darius relief at Naqš-e Rustam. He may also be depicted in the relief at Bisitun. He was among the seven Persian nobles involved in overthrowing Bardiya/Gaumata, and had close family links with Darius. Gobryas became Darius' father-in-law, when Darius married his daughter before he became king (**108**), and he himself married a sister of Darius (Hdt.7.5.1; for the marriage alliances of Darius I see below **177**). His son Mardonius married a daughter of Darius, Artozostre (**179**). This inscription defines him as a member of the Persian tribe of the Patischorians, who are also mentioned in Strabo 15.3.1. It has been suggested that the word 'Patischorian' means '(region) lying against the sun, sunny-side slope'.

113 Aspathines, the Bow-bearer, holds the battle-axe of Darius the King.

DNd

114 Tell Akkaya, Aspathines spoke as follows:
'60 quarts of flour are to be issued as rations to Zimakka, a *sitmaka* person, assigned to the king as an irrigation worker(?), in year 28, at Persepolis. 13 days in month 4, 30 days in month 5, 17 days in month 6, for a total of 60 days, he receives monthly 30 quarts of flour.'
Puktezza wrote the text.
Mirina communicated the message. (PTS 14)

PF 1853

115 Tell Baradkama, the treasurer, Aspathines speaks as follows:
'357 karsha 9 " shekels of silver are to be issued to workers subsisting on rations at Persepolis whose apportionments are set by Mauš. They are Hattian workers on the columned hall.
Sheep and wine are given equally.1 sheep (equals) 3 shekels, and 10 quarts of wine equal 1 shekel of silver. For months seven to twelve, in total 6 months of year 2, the decurion and (the members of) the decury receive (rations).
84 men, each receiving each month 3 shekels of silver, are receiving (it). 57 men, each receiving each month 2 shekels of silver, are receiving (it). 74 men, each receiving each month 1 shekel 3/4 of silver, are receiving (it). 19 men each per month (receive) 1 shekel and 1/4 of a shekel of silver they receive. 79 men each per month receive 1 shekel of silver, they are receiving (it). Total 313 workers.'
Month 4, year 3.
The sealed document has been received. Dadda wrote the message.
He received the *dumme* from Šakka. (PTS 14)

PT 12

In the relief at Naqš-e Rustam Aspathines wears Median dress, consisting of a large coat fastened with a belt, riding trousers and a rounded hat. He carries a large *gorytus*, which includes a bow-case and a quiver. The name 'Aspathines' is the Greek rendering of the Persian name Aspačana (Elam. *Ašbazana*), which translates as 'delighting in horses'. Aspathines is attested in texts from Persepolis as a high Persian official who served under Darius I and is attested until the third year of Xerxes' reign. Aspathines carried his own personal seal, bearing the Elamite inscription 'Ašbaza(na), son of Pani[...]pi' (PTS 14*). Herodotus erroneously names him as one of the seven nobles (Hdt.3.70; see above **38**), confusing him with Ardumaniš (**44**: §68). Possibly Ardumaniš had died during or after Gaumata's revolt and Ašbazana took his place among the seven nobles. Aspathines' son Prexaspes was an admiral in Xerxes' fleet in 480 (Hdt.7.97).

Aspathines is attested as an official in the Persepolis administration, dictating letter orders which allow the withdrawal of rations for individuals. The letters are signed with his personal seal, PTS 14, reflecting his high status. A *dumme* may have been a copy of the document.

The King's Benefactors and Friends

116 Syloson (*the brother of Polycrates of Samos*) then learned that the successor to the throne was the man to whom, at his request, he had given the garment in Egypt. So he went up to Susa and sat at the king's porch, saying that he was one of Darius' benefactors.

Herodotus 3.140.1

117 [85.2] I could record many names of Ionian ships' captains who captured Greek ships; but I will speak of none save Theomestor son of Androdamas and Phylacus son of Histiaeus, both Samians. [85.3] I make mention of these two alone because Theomestor was for this feat of arms made tyrant of Samos by the Persians, and Phylacus was recorded among the king's benefactors and given much land. These benefactors of the king are called in the Persian language *orosangae*.

Herodotus 8.85.2–3

118 [27.4] Alexander (*III, the Great*) now put two hipparchs in charge of the Companions. Hephaestion son of Amyntor and Clitus son of Dropides, and after dividing the Companions' brigade into two parts, since he would not have wished a single man, though his closest friend, to command so large a body of cavalry, especially as it was the best of all his mounted force in reputation and valour, he arrived among the people formerly called Ariaspians, but later also nicknamed Benefactors, because they assisted Cyrus (*II*) son of Cambyses (*I*) in his Scythian expedition.

Arrian, *Anabasis* 3.27.4

119 [28.2] 'As soon as I learned that you were coming down to the Greek sea, I desired to offer you money for the war, and I enquired into the matter, and my reckoning showed that I had two thousand talents of silver, and of gold four million Daric staters lacking seven thousand. [28.3] All this I freely give to you; for myself, I make sufficient livelihood from my slaves and my estates.' Xerxes was pleased with what he (*the Lydian Pythius*) had said and replied: [29.1] 'My Lydian friend, since I left Persia, I have met no-one who offered hospitality to my army, nor anyone who came out of his own free will before me to offer money for the war, except you. You have provided greatly for my army and offered me great sums of money. [29.2] In return I will therefore give you this: I make you my friend, and to complete your four million staters, I will give you seven thousand staters, so that your four million may not lack seven thousand staters, but you may have the full amount through my completing it.'

Herodotus 7.28.2–29.2

120 Concerning the sons of Spitamas, Cyrus (*II*) appointed Spitakes as satrap of the Derbikae and Megabernes as satrap of the Barcanians. He commanded them to obey their mother in all respects; then he made Amorges (*the Scythian king*) their friend by putting their right hands into each other's. He drank to the well-being of those (of them) who remained loyal to their reciprocal good will, and to the misfortune of those who would undertake disloyal actions.

Ctesias *FGrH* 688 F9

The King's Benefactors and Friends were individuals or groups of people who had proved their devotion to the king through their service or acts of loyalty. While Greek texts distinguish between benefactors (*euergetai*) and friends (*philoi*), it is difficult to detect a difference between these statuses. Both were rewarded with special royal gifts and enjoyed a privileged status with the king; quite possibly the terms 'benefactor' and the 'friend' were used interchangeably.

The most famous benefactor was probably Otanes, who received annual gifts from Darius (**121**). Records of their names were kept in the royal archives, and Herodotus refers to Phylacus' name being added to this list (**117**). The noble Lydian Pythius was rewarded for his generosity towards Xerxes' army, and became a King's Friend. As Ctesias suggests, the bond of friendship seems to have been struck through holding the friend's right hand. The term *orosangae*, which Herodotus claims is a Persian word, may be derived from an Old Iranian word **varu- sanha-*, 'wide-famed, whose praise is widespread'.

Coinage had been invented by the Lydians *c*.600. The Persian coin called Daric was introduced by Darius I, though according to Xenophon it was already used at the time of Cyrus II (Xen.*Cyr*.5.2.7). The name derives from the Old Persian word for 'gold', *daranya*. The standard weight for the gold coin was 8.41 grams. As illustrated below, the coin depicted a 'running archer', a man dressed in the Persian long dress, holding his bow and arrow ready to shoot with one knee bent as if in motion.

11. Daric coin

Gift-giving

121 [84.1] The rest of the Seven then deliberated on what was the fairest way of appointing a king, and they resolved that, if another of the Seven than Otanes should gain the royal power, Otanes and all his descendants should receive as a mark of honour an annual gift of a Median robe and all such presents as the Persians hold most precious.

Herodotus 3.84.1

122 [2.7] Though he (*Cyrus II*) far exceeded all other men in the amount of revenues he received, yet he excelled still more in the quantity of presents he gave. It was Cyrus, therefore, who began the practice of lavish giving, and among the kings it continues even to this day. [2.8] For who has richer friends to show than the Persian king? Who is there that is known to adorn his friends with more beautiful robes than does the king? Whose gifts are so readily recognised as some of those that the king gives, such as bracelets, necklaces, and horses with gold-studded bridles? For, as everybody knows, no one over there is allowed to have such things except those to whom the king has given them.

Xenophon, *Cyropaedia* 8.2.7–8

The royal practice of gift-giving served to reward noble Persians for their service to the king and at the same time ensured their loyalty and support. A royal gift was a great honour for a Persian, but the continued loyalty of the recipient was expected in return. The most precious gift was a Median robe, given to Otanes and to the Cilician king Syennesis (Xen. *An*.1.2.27). Different pieces of jewellery, crafted in the royal Achaemenid style, identified the special status of the recipient amongst other Persian nobles. In addition to the honour of receiving material gifts, there were also cases in which the king, as a symbol of his recognition of a noble's loyalty, offered one of his daughters in marriage. (For Themistocles receiving gifts from the king see above **82**.)

3.2. THE ADMINISTRATION OF THE EMPIRE
Satraps and satrapies

123 Darius the king says: '(There is) a country, Margiana by name, that rebelled against me. There was one man, Frada by name, a Margian, they made him their chief. After that I sent a Persian, Dadaršiš by name, my subject, satrap of Bactria, against him.'

44: §38

124 Darius the king says: 'That Vahyazdata who called himself Bardiya had sent forth an army to Arachosia against a Persian, Vivana by name, my subject, satrap of Arachosia, and he (*Vahyazdata*) had made one man their commander.'

44: §45

125 This Aryandes had been appointed satrap (Gr. *hyparchos*) of Egypt by Cambyses (*II*), but at a later date was killed for trying to make himself equal to Darius.

Herodotus 4.166.1

126 Because of their enthusiastic allegiance he (*Cyrus II*) never sent a Persian satrap to govern either the Cilicians or the Cyprians, but was always satisfied with their native rulers. Tribute, however, he did receive from them, and whenever he needed forces he made a requisition upon them for troops.

Xenophon, *Cyropaedia* 7.4.2

127 When he (*Cyrus II*) arrived in Babylon, he decided to send satraps to govern the nations he had subdued. But he wished the commanders of the garrisons in the citadels and the colonels in command of the guards throughout the country to be responsible to no one but himself. He made this provision intending that if any of the satraps, on the strength of the wealth or the men at their command, should break out into open insolence or attempt to refuse obedience (Gr. *proskynesis*), they might at once find opposition in their province.

Xenophon, *Cyropaedia* 8.6.1

The lands of the Persian empire were administered as provinces, or satrapies, headed by a satrap. The word 'satrap' derives from an Old Persian word *xšaçapāvan*, which literally means 'protector of the realm'. The term is known to us from the Bisitun Inscription (**44**: §§38, 45). Herodotus uses the word 'satrap' alongside the word *hyparchos*.

Near Eastern and Greek sources show that satraps had already been appointed at the time of Cyrus II and Cambyses II. Cyrus had installed Gobryas as governor of Babylonia (**11**: III.20), first Tabalus (**16**) and then Oroites (Hdt.3.120.1) as satrap of Sardis, and Mitrobates as satrap of Dascylium (Hdt.3.126.2). Cambyses appointed Aryandes as satrap of Egypt (**125**), who was eventually succeeded by Arsames after the revolt of Inaros in 460-454 (**88**). As a rule, this important office was given only to Persian nobles, who often were relatives of the king. Certain regions, like Cilicia, Caria, Lycia, and Cyprus, were administered by local dynasts, while some cities in Asia Minor and Phoenicia were ruled by city-kings. A range of high officials, administrative, legal and military, would be employed in the service of a satrap, ensuring the collection and recording of the tribute, the recording of legal affairs, and the security of the satrapy. The satrap's loyalty to the king was crucial for the existence of the empire. Disloyalty was punished severely, as happened in the case of Masistes, the brother of Xerxes, who attempted a revolt in Bactria (Hdt.9.113), and in the case of Aryandes, the satrap of Egypt, who overstepped his authority when he minted his own coins (**125**). As a sign of respect, satraps, as well as other nobles, had to perform the *proskynesis*, the gesture of obedience, to the king. In the audience scene in the relief from Persepolis it is identified as the gesture made by the Persian approaching the king, who is seated on his throne. The Persian is bowing to the king, holding his right hand in front of his mouth as a sign of respect. Others suggest that *proskynesis* meant a complete prostration before the king, having to fall down before him (for *proskynesis* as part of Persian customs see Hdt.1.134.1).

The *pihātu*

128   2″ minas and 2″ shekels of white lower quality silver of one-eighth alloy, belonging to (the woman) Abesukku the daughter of Rimut, owed by Bel-iddina son of Itti-Bel-lummir the son of Mušezib.
The house which is next to the house of Šamaš-pir'u-usur son of Marduk-šumu-ibni, and next to the house of Belšunu is the pledge of Abesukku. There shall be no rent for the house and no [interest] on the silver. Until the appointed time(?) the house is at the disposal of Abesukku; she will live in it. She will renew the roof and will carry out the repair work to the foundation walls.
From the first day of the month Simanu, year 20 of Darius, the house is at Abesukku's disposal. Three staircases, large and small, are at her disposal until the appointed time.
Witnesses: Bel-iddin son of Apla of the Sin-i[li] family; Nabu-ittannu son of Gu[...]; [...]-ippu son of Linuh-libbi-ili; [... son of Na]bu-zeru-lišir of the Šangu-ea family; Nabu-[... son of L]abaši; Muranu son of Basi[ja of the Sin()?]-ili family; Ea-kasir son of Ra[...of the E]teru family; Iddin-Bel son of Nidintu; [...]anu son of Bel-remanni of the Sin-ili family; Bel-mudammiq son of Bel-nasir of the Sin-damaqu family; Eriba-Marduk son of Balatu of the A[...] family; Bel-etiranni the slave of Ta[ttannu] the governor of Across-the-River.
Scribe: Bel-aplu-iddina son of Bel-nasir of the Sin-damaqu family.
Babylon, 23 Ayyaru, year 20 (*5 June 502*) of Darius (*II*), king of Babylon, king of lands.

VS 4 152

129   Then Zerubbabel, son of Shealtiel, and Jeshua, son of Jozadak, set to work to rebuild the house of God in Jerusalem. And the prophets of God were with them, helping them. At that time, Tattenai, governor of Across-the-River, and Shethar-Bozenai (*Satibarzanes*) and their associates went to them and asked: "Who authorised you to rebuild this temple and restore this structure?" They also asked: "What are the names of the men constructing this building?" But the eye of their God was watching over the elders of the Jews, and they were not stopped until a report should go to Darius (*I*) and his written reply be received.

Ezra 5.2–5

Tattenai (Bab. *Tattannu*) was governor of the region of Across-the-River (Syria-Palestine). As a governor (Bab. *pihātu*), his office may have been equal, or perhaps subordinate, to that of the satrap of the whole province of Babylon and Across-the-River. **128**, dated to 502, confirms that Tattenai was in office during the reign of Darius I. The passage from *Ezra* shows that he had authority over affairs in the Persian province of Judah. In his letter to the Persian king, he enquired about the original document issued by Cyrus II authorising the rebuilding of the temple in Jerusalem, ensuring that the Jewish community had permission to carry out the building work (see also below **201–205**).

130 On the instructions of Huta[...], son of Pagakanna, the governor of Babylon and Across-the-River, and of Lilut, the brother of Adad-ibni, the scribe (and) chancellor, and of Gadalama, son of Banna-Ea, the scribe (and) chancellor, Siha, son of Ahulap, the overseer of the work-house of [...], has received 14 *kur* of barley from Iddin-Bel, son of Iqiša-Marduk, descendant of Šangu-šamaš. Siha will enter the aforesaid 14 *kur* of barley in the crown ledger as (payment credited to) Iddin-Bel, son of Iqiša-Marduk, descendant of Šangu-šamaš.

Witnesses: Nabu-ah-ittannu, son of Nabu-eriba, descendant of Rab-bani; Bel-kasir, son of Remūt, descendant of Arad-Nergal; Bel-etir, son of Beni-zeri; [...]-ittannu, son of Iddin-Nabu, descendant of (...); [..-ubal]lissu, son of Bel-ahhe-iqiša, descendant of [...]; Ahušunu, son of Bel-ahhe-iddin, descendant of [...]-Marduk(?); Mušezib-Marduk, son of Marduk-šar-usur.

Scribe: Ahhe-iddin, son of Nabu-iddin.

Babylon, month 6, day 24, year 36 (*5 October 486*) (of) Darius (I), king of Babylon and the lands.

Siha has received the entire (payment of) barley according to (?) [...].

BM 74554; Stolper 1989

The Babylonian text, documenting the transfer of 14 *kur* of barley from Iddin-Bel to Siha in Babylon, mentions a governor of Babylon and Across-the-River, who is otherwise unknown in our sources. His name is only partially preserved as Huta-[...] the son of Pagakanna. He can be identified as a successor to Gobryas, who had been installed as governor in Babylonia in 535 by Cyrus II (see **11**: III:20,). The date places him at the end of the reign of Darius I.

The *saris*

131 Year 36 of the Good God (*486*), lord of the Two Lands, Darius, endowed with life like Re, beloved of Min the Great who lives at Koptos.

Written by the *saris* of Persia, Atiyawahy, son of Arsames, born of the lady Qandjou.

Posener 1936: no.24

132 Min the Great, who is placed on (his) altar.

Year 10 of the Lord of the Two Lands (*476*), Xerxes.

Made by the *saris* of Persia, Atiyawahy and Ariyawrata.

Posener 1936: no.27

The Persian official Atiyawahy, son of Arsames and Qandjou, was probably the governor of Wadi Hammamat. Atiyawahy is also attested as having been in charge of a group of workers who procured building material for the construction of the temple at el-Khargeh in the quarries of Wadi Hammamat. His title, '*saris*', may be derived from the Akkadian title '*ša rēš šarri*', and may be translated as 'master' or 'governor'. Egyptian inscriptions attest the activities of Atiyawahy in Koptos from the sixth year of Cambyses' reign to the thirteenth year of the reign of Xerxes (524–473). For Ariyawrata see **79f**.

The peoples of the empire

133 §1.I am Darius, the Great King, king of kings, king of many countries, son of Hystaspes, an Achaemenid.

§2. Darius the king says: 'By the favour of Ahura Mazda these are the countries which I received into my possession along with this Persian people, who feared me and who brought me tribute: Elam, Media, Babylonia, Arabia, Assyria, Egypt, Armenia, Cappadocia, Sardis, Ionians who are on the mainland, and those who are by the sea, Sagartia, Parthia, Drangiana, Aria, Bactria, Sogdiana, Chorasmia, Sattagydia, Arachosia, Sind, Gandara, Scythia, Maka.'

§3. Darius the king says: 'If you should think: "May I not fear anybody", protect the Persian people. If the Persian people are protected, continuous happiness for a very long time will come down towards this house.'

DPe

134 §1. Darius, the Great King, king of kings, king of countries, son of Hystaspes, an Achaemenid.

§2. Darius the king says: 'This is the kingdom which I hold: from the Scythians who are beyond Sogdiana to Ethiopia, from Sind to Sardis. (The kingdom) which Ahura Mazda, the greatest of the gods, bestowed upon me. May Ahura Mazda protect me and my royal house.'

DPh

135 Xerxes the king says: 'By the favour of Ahura Mazda these are the countries of which I am king outside Persia. I ruled over them, they brought me tribute, they did what I told them. My law held them firm: Media, Elam, Arachosia, Armenia, Drangiana, Parthia, Aria, Bactria, Sogdiana, Chorasmia, Babylonia, Assyria, Sattagydia, Sardis, Egypt, Ionians—those who dwell by the sea, and those who dwell across the sea—men of Maka, Arabia, Gandara, Sind, Cappadocia, Dahae, Amyrgian Scythians, pointed-cap Scythians, Skudra, men of Akaufaka, Libyans, Carians, Ethiopians.'

191: §3

Darius' five lists of the lands of the Persian empire (**44**: §6, **46**: §3; **48**: §3, **133**: §2, and **134**: §2), all differ slightly from each other. The most general, DPh, found in Persepolis, was inscribed in three languages on a gold plate and on a silver one, which are now in the Archaeological Museum in Tehran. Darius simply manifests the extent of his empire North to South and East to West. An empire as vast as the Persian empire, stretching West to East from Egypt and the eastern Mediterranean to India, and North to South from the Caucasus to the Persian Gulf, was unprecedented in the ancient Near East. When we speak of the empire of Alexander the Great, we should know that the extent of that empire had been established by the end of the sixth century BC.

The earliest of these inscriptions, the Bisitun Inscription (**44**: §6), lists 23 lands. In effect they reflect the kingdoms and lands conquered by Cyrus II and Cambyses II, since the inscription was carved immediately after Darius' succession to the throne, probably in 519. Darius states his possession of these lands as a *status quo*, but it is curious that he passes (deliberately?) over the fact that the previous kings established the Persian empire. The inscription DPe, written only in Old Persian on the outer south wall of the royal terrace of Persepolis, also lists 23 countries, though with slight variations. Most notably Darius distinguishes between the Ionians who live by the sea, meaning the Greeks of Asia Minor, and the Greeks of the mainland, meaning those who had offered earth and water to the king and had therefore officially acknowledged his authority as Persian king (**57** and **58**). The inscription leaves out Persis, while Sind (*India*), which had been conquered some time during Darius' reign, is now added. Unfortunately, no sources have survived to tell us about the conquest of India.

48: §3, the inscription on the tomb façade at Naqš-e Rustam, repeats the list of lands of **46**: §3, including 29 lands and distinguishing between different ethnic groups of Scythians. Finally, Xerxes' list, which is part of the *daiva*-inscription (**191**), includes thirty-one lands, adding an unknown region, Akaufaka, and the land of the Dahae.

Despite the variations, all inscriptions list the Persian lands in a similar order, beginning with the core lands of the empire, Media, Elam and Babylon, and then moving geographically to the lands around these core lands. The absence of a strict order indicates that these lists do not reflect clearly defined administrative regions. By listing the different countries the kings want to demonstrate the extent and the power of the empire. Each of these lands was inhabited by a vast number of different ethnic groups, who all spoke different languages and dialects. The royal inscriptions were intended to document each individual group of people, or accurately record the bureaucratic units in which these peoples were doubtless administered.

Tribute, gifts, and taxes

136 Darius the king says: 'By the favour of Ahura Mazda these are the countries, which I seized outside Persia: I ruled over them, they brought me tribute (OP *bāji*). They did what I told them. My law held them firm. (...)'

46: §3

137 28 rams, 4 male lambs, 392 ewes, 46 (female) yearlings, 6 female lambs, total 476 sheep, (were) entrusted to (the man) Miššumanya, alive, (as) tax (Elam. *baziš*). Year 17.

PF 267

138 Tell Parnaka that Raubasa and his companions spoke as follows: 'May god and king become your *širi*! [...] now we have taken small cattle at the sheepfolds. We have sent the tax-handlers (Elam. *bazi uttibe*) to you. We have sent Umizza son of Halpa. He lives in Hiran in (the district) called Halkukaptarriš. We have entrusted (the small cattle) to him, a herdsman of the king, (for) whom Harena does the apportioning, his *ansara* (official) (is) Miššumanaya. (At) the sheepfold of (the place) Rautannuš, (at) Kamzarasaš (in the district?) called Rautaš, (for) Šuddayauda the chief of workers to apportion. At that sheepfold they are stabled(?).

From Teyauka: 2 (male) goats, 2 (female) goats, 1 ewe—(in) total 5 small cattle of his.

And from Datezza(?): 2 (male) goats, 2 (female) goats, 1 female kid—(in) total 5 small cattle of his.

And from (the woman) Madamiš: 7 (female) goats, 1 ewe—(in) total 8 small cattle of hers.

And from Bawuk[...]: 2 (male) goats, 2 (female) goats, 5 ewes—(in) total 9 small cattle of his.

And from Mauruza, a *rara* worker of the king, (his) apportioner (being) Kambezza: 5 (male) goats, 10 (female) goats—(in) total 15 small cattle of his.

And from Mirakama, the treasurer, (his) apportioner (being) Karkiš: 6 (female) goats—(in) total 6.

Of men living (at) Hiran we took: a total of 11 (male) goats, a total of 29 (female) goats, a total of 1 female kid, a total of 7 ewes—(in) total 48 small cattle.

Year18, month 1, (day) 21 [...] we sent(?) the tax-handlers to you [...].

PF 2070

139 Persis is the only country which I did not record as paying tribute (*phoros*); for the Persians are exempt from paying taxes.

Herodotus 3.97.1

In the royal inscriptions, the Persian king lists the lands of the empire which bring tribute to the king. Absent from the list of lands is Persis, the centre of Persian royal rule. Yet while Herodotus understands this to mean that Persis was exempt from paying taxes, the Persepolis Fortification texts clearly record the tax payments of the Persians in the administrative districts of Persis. Tax-collectors were sent out to collect the taxes which were paid in the form of livestock, and which were then recorded on the clay tablets (**137, 138**). There must then be a difference between the payment of tribute and the payment of taxes. Tribute was paid by the peoples in the satrapies of the empire. This was probably an amount valued individually for each country that brought tribute, though no record from Near Eastern sources survives to tell us how large the amount was for each satrapy or when this amount was paid. It is likely that the tribute was collected by the satrap, and that most of the amount was taken to the royal palace, while a percentage may have remained at the satrapal centre to cover expenses there.

The royal inscriptions use the Old Persian term *bāji* to refer to the tribute. Yet *bāji* not only means the fixed payment to be paid by the peoples who were subjects of the king, but also includes payments made in the form of gifts. For example, neither the Nubians nor the Colchians paid tribute, nor did the Arabs, who were thus rewarded for their support of Cambyses' campaigns against Egypt, but these peoples are named in the royal inscriptions and are also depicted on the Great Staircase of the Audience Hall of Persepolis, bearing gifts for the king. The question who pays tribute and who brings gifts is best answered with the observation that those peoples who were at the borders of the Persian empire, in charge of defending them from invading tribes, as well as the nomadic tribes of the Zagros mountains, enjoyed a semi-autonomous status within the Persian empire. As long as they acknowledged the authority of the Persian king and did not contest his rule, and expressed their respect for the king by the annual bringing of gifts, these peoples could continue to live in this kind of semi-independence.

Thus, *bāji* incorporates gifts as well as tribute. Herodotus' distinction between the two, referring to them as *phoros* and *dora* respectively, is slightly misleading, as 'gifts' also were an expected kind of payment to the king. As Persis proper was the centre of the Persian empire and the Persians therefore not a tribute-paying subject people, Persis itself indeed did not have to pay tribute, but it was not exempt from paying taxes to the king.

The lists of lands given in the royal inscriptions differ considerably from the tribute list provided by Herodotus. What is their proper meaning? No Persian source has survived which would allow us to determine which lands paid tribute or how high the contribution of each land was. This leaves Herodotus as our only source giving an idea of the fiscal organisation of the empire and the amount of tribute each land or group of peoples had to pay. According to Herodotus' list, the Persian empire is divided into twenty regions, each comprising one or more lands or peoples who jointly pay a fixed sum of tribute to the king. His list divides the empire as follows:

1. The Ionians and the Asiatic Magnesians, Aeolians, Carians, Lycians and Milyans, and the Pamphylians paid 400 talents of silver.
2. The Mysians, Lydians, Lasonians, Cabalaians, Hytennians paid 500 talents (of silver).
3. The people from the Hellespont, on the right hand side of the straits as you sail in, and the Phrygians, Thracians of Asia, Paphlagonians, Mariandynians, and Syrians paid 360 talents (of silver).
4. The Cilicians paid 500 talents of silver and 360 white horses.
5. The Phoenicians, Syria-Palestine, and Cyprus paid 350 talents. Exempted from tribute are the Arabians.
6. Egypt, which includes the regions of Libya, Cyrene, and Barca, paid 700 talents, revenue from fishing, and 120,000 bushels of grain, which were to be provided for the Persians stationed at the fort at Memphis.
7. The Sattagydians, Gandarians, Dadicaeans, and Aparytaeans paid 170 talents.
8. The people of Susa and the Cissians paid 300 talents.
9. Babylon and Assyria paid 1,000 talents of silver and brought 500 boys to be eunuchs.
10. The Medians, Paricanians, and Orthocorybantians paid 450 talents.
11 The Caspians, Pausicaeans, Pantimathians, Daritaeans paid 200 talents.
12. Bactria brought 360 talents.
13. Pactyica and Armenia 400 talents.
14. The Sagartians, Sarangians, Thamanaeans, Utians, Mycians, and the southern islands brought 600 talents.
15. The Scythians and Caspians 250 talents.
16. The Parthians, Chorasmians and the peoples from Sogdiana and Aria paid 300 talents.
17. The Paricanians and Asian Ethiopians paid 400 talents.
18. The Matienians, Saspirians, and Alarodians paid 200 talents.
19. The Moschians, Tibarenians, Macrones, Mossynoecians and Mares paid 300 talents.
20. India brought 360 talents of gold dust.

Herodotus lists twenty provinces (Hdt.3.89–94), as opposed to varying numbers of the lands given in the Persian royal inscriptions. In fact Herodotus' list refers to the administrative and fiscal districts of the empire and cannot be taken as a list of satrapies. Within the listing of the group of peoples of the empire Herodotus' list fails to mention the lands of Cappadocia and Arachosia. While he lists the lands of Sattagydia, Gandara, Drangiana (Sarangians), Parthia, Chorasmia, Sogdiana and Aria in groups with one another, these lands are listed separately in the Bisitun Inscription.

High officials and workers of Persepolis
Parnaka

140 Parnaka received as rations 20 sheep, supplied by the man Umaka. For a period of 10 days, he daily received 2 sheep. Year 20, month 12.
Marriyakarša wrote the text. Mannunda communicated the message. (PFS 9)

PF 662

141 Parnaka received as rations 90 quarts of wine, entrusted to Karkiš. For a period of one day, at a village named Hadarakkaš.
Hišbeš wrote the text. Mannunda communicated its message. Year 23, month 2, day 25, the sealed document was delivered. (PFS 16)

PF 665

142 Parnaka received as rations 3,960 quarts of flour, entrusted to Upirradda, at Persepolis. For a period of 22 days, every day, 180 quarts of flour were received (by him). Year 23, month 5.
Irtena wrote the text. Mannunda communicated the message. (PFS 16)

PF 668

143 Tell Maraza the wine-carrier, Parnaka spoke as follows:
'55 quarts of wine are to be issued as their rations to Babylonian scribes assigned by me. For the ninth month, year 23, 11 men receive 5 quarts per month each.'
(In) Year 23, month 9, this sealed document was delivered.
Takmaziya wrote it. He received the *dumme* from Yauna.(PFS 16)

PF 1807

At the end of the sixth century Parnaka was the highest official at Persepolis, working as the chief economic administrator. He executes the orders of the king and members of the royal family, communicating their requests to the appropriate officials (see **159–161**). He is one of the few officials, apart from the king himself, who authorises the travel rations of individuals and ration payments for workers. His high status is reflected in the quantity of provisions he receives at Persepolis. His daily ration consists of 90 quarts of wine, 180 quarts of flour, and 2 sheep. Parnaka's orders are communicated to the appropriate official through a letter, dictated to a scribe. The letter contains details about the monthly ration for a work group. The different kinds of food - wine or beer, grain and meat - issued to a work force are always listed separately, as each foodstuff is kept in a different storeroom, and each storeroom accounts for its deliveries separately. The seal on the letter identifies Parnaka as the official who authorises the letter order to be carried out. In Parnaka's case, there are two seals, PFS 9 and PFS 16, which comes into use after 500: Parnaka states in two letters dated to June 500 (PF 2067, PF 2068) that the previous seal is being replaced by the new one: 'The seal that formerly (was) mine has been replaced. Now this seal that has been applied (to) this tablet (is) mine' (PF 2068: ll.11-14). Most interesting is the name of the office worker, Yauna, which means 'Ionian'. While other texts state that Ionians worked as labourers in Persepolis (see **45**: §4), this text indicates that Ionian Greeks could be employed carrying out secretarial work in the Persian administration.

The inscription of Parnaka's seal (PFS 9) identifies him as 'Parnaka, son of Arsames'. This Arsames was the grandfather of Darius (see **44**: § 1), which means that Parnaka was the brother of Darius' father Hystaspes, and thereby Darius' uncle. He might well be the father of Artabazos (see Hdt.7.66) and the great-great-grandfather of Pharnabazos (see **111**).

Ziššawiš

144 240 quarts of flour entrusted to Miduš were received as rations by Ziššawiš. For a period of four days at Dašer. Month 8, year 18.
Kurdumiš wrote the text. He received the *dumme* from Ribaya. (PFS 83)

PF 671

145 Ziššawiš received as rations 90 quarts of wine supplied by Muška. For a period of 3 days, at Parmadan and Pirradaše(?). Month 9, year 18.
Hintamukka wrote the text, He received the *dumme* from Ribaya. (PFS 83)

PF 673

146 Ziššawiš received as rations 90 sheep, supplied by Kampiya. In the tenth and eleventh months, for a total of 2 months, he receives 1″ sheep daily. Year 19.
Hintamukka wrote the text. He received the *dumme* from Ripiš. (PFS 11)

PF 678

Ziššawiš was Parnaka's second-in-command. He has been identified with Tithaeus, known from Herodotus (7.88.1). His son is Datis, who commanded the expedition of 490 against Athens and Eretria (see **59**). Ziššawiš' daily ration of 30 quarts of wine, 60 quarts of flour, and 1″ sheep, reflects a lower rank than Parnaka's.

Chief of Workers, law-officers and accountants

147 Šiyatiparna (received) 450 quarts of flour supplied by Medumannuš, at the estate (where) Iršena, the chief of workers (Elam. *kurdabatiš*), the Anshanite, does the apportioning. He gave it to Tamukkan workers of (the man) Minmira, whom he took to Tamukkan.
304 workers daily receive each 1″ quarts of flour. For a period of 1 day they received (it). Year 22, month 6, they received these rations.

PF 1368

148 Tell Iršena, the chief of workers, Parnaka spoke as follows:
'150 quarts of flour from Persepolis (are) to be issued as rations to Addarnuriš the Assyrian who handles cedar wood (at) Persepolis. Rations for the third, fourth, fifth, sixth, (and) seventh months, for a total period of 5 months. Year 24. Month per month he receives 30 quarts.'
Šamanda wrote the text. He received the *dumme* from Yauna.
Year 24, month 5, the sealed document was delivered. (PFS 16)

PF 1799

149 Bakabada the law officer (Elam. *dattibarra*, OP **dāta-bara*) of Parnaka received 20 quarts of beer. He carried a sealed document of Parnaka. The rations were for 20 days. Year 23, month 9.

PF 1272

150 Ištiba(?) the law officer received 21 quarts of flour supplied by Haturdada. 6 gentlemen receive 1″ quarts. 12 servants receive one quart.
He carried a sealed document of the king. Year 21.

PF 1307

151 Dattanna the auditor (Elam. *halnut haššira*) received as rations 300 quarts of flour supplied by Parru. Dattanna is receiving daily 2 quarts. 3 servant boys are receiving daily 1 quart. For a period of 2 months they received (it). He carried a sealed document of Bakabana. Year 19.

PF 1240

152 Dattanna the accountant (Elam. *mušin zikkira*) received (as) rations (for) 6 days 6 quarts of beer supplied by Ummanna. He carried a sealed document of the king. Month10, year 22.

PF 1274

A number of officials served in the administration of Persepolis, immediately subordinate to the highest official, Parnaka. One of these was Iršena, who himself issued orders sealed with his personal seal (PFS 4). In addition to his title, 'chief of workers', the text also provides a detail about Iršena's background, stating that he came from Anshan, the former Elamite capital northwest of Persepolis. The expenditure of food rations was controlled by Parnaka, who gave his orders for issuing rations to Iršena through a letter. Iršena himself would then delegate the order further down the administrative line, to be passed on to the appropriate storehouse. The law-officers and accountants were sent out into the districts to ensure that law and order were maintained and that legal and administrative transactions were properly recorded. These officials likewise were answerable to Parnaka.

The work force in Persis

153 1 woman chief (Elam. *arašṧara*) of the (female) *pašap* (-workers) subsisting on rations at (the place) Umpuranuš, whose apportionments are set by Iršena, received as rations 30 quarts of wine supplied by Irtuppiya. Month 2, year 22.

PF 876

154 (Female) *pašap* (-workers) at Liduma, assigned by Iršena, subsisting on rations, received as rations for one month 2, 615 quarts of grain supplied by Irtuppiya. Month 5, year 21.
16 men (each receive) 30 quarts, 7 boys 20, 5 boys 15, 6 boys 10. 1 woman 50 (quarts), 34 women 40, 9 women 30, 1 woman 20. 2 girls 20, 2 girls 15, 9 girls 10. Total 92 workers.

PF 847

Any woman employed as an *arašṧara* received one of the highest ration payments among the workers in Persis. Her standard ration consisted of 30 quarts of wine, 50 quarts of grain and 4 sheep per year. The *arašṧara* (pl. *arašṧarap*) headed the work force of predominantly female *pašap*-workers, who are attested in numerous towns and villages in Persis. **154** shows that women could receive higher rations than male workers. The one woman receiving 50 quarts of grain is probably the *arašṧara* of this group. The different ration scales indicate that these workers carried out specialised labour, which was paid according to the level of qualification. The term *pašap* probably describes a particular type of workforce, rather than a specific occupation. A convincing translation of this term has not yet been provided. For Liduma see on **168**.

155 Cappadocian workers, subsisting on rations, received as rations (at) Baktiš, (for) 1 month 1,070 quarts of grain supplied by Turpiš from the place Kurištiš. Month 1, year 23.
19 men (each received) 30 (quarts), 6 boys 10. 19 women 20 (quarts), 6 girls 10. Total 50 workers.

PF 850

156 Tell Upirradda, Zišṧawiš spoke as follows:
'2,240 quarts of grain are to be issued as rations to Babylonian workers subsisting on rations, grain-handlers at (the place) Barniš, whose apportionments are set by Takšena. In month 3, for one month, year 23, 6 men each receive 30 quarts, 36 boys each 20 quarts, 18 boys each 15 quarts, 5 boys each 10 quarts, 21 women 20 quarts, 25 girls each 15 quarts, 3 girls each 10 quarts. Total 124 workers.'
Hintamukka wrote it. Kamezza communicated the message. He received the *dumme* from Hitibel. (PFS 11)

PF 1821

Labour which required little or no qualification was paid a standard ration of 30 quarts of grain for men and 20 quarts for women. The text identifies the ethnic origin of this work group as Cappadocian. It is possible that labour was carried out by whole families who came from particular villages.

Special rations for mothers

157 20 quarts of grain supplied by Šarukba, were received and were given to Lanunu, a woman (who) bore a male baby.

10 quarts of grain were received and (were given) to Parrukkuzziš, a woman (who) bore a female baby.

They were given to a total of 2 *post partum* women. Manzaturruš and his companions received and gave it to them. Year 23, month 4. (At) Tikrakkaš.

PF 1226

158 Lanunu, a woman (who) bore a male baby, received 10 quarts of wine, supplied by Irkezza.

Parrukkuzziš, a woman (who) bore a female baby, received 5 quarts of wine.

They were given to a total of 2 *post partum* women. Manzaturruš and his companions received it and gave it to them. Year 23, month 4. (At) Tikrakkaš.

PF-NN 358

Special rations were given out to groups of workers or individuals. Among this group are women who had just given birth to a child. The two texts above name the same two women, Lanunu and Parrukkuzziš, who gave birth to a boy and a girl respectively. For one month they receive an extra ration of foodstuffs, a combination of grain and wine. Women who gave birth to a boy received twice the amount of foodstuffs that those who gave birth to a girl received. The almost equal number of births of girls and boys, and the evidence for girls and boys in the work force in Persis, argue against infanticide of girls.

3.3. ROYAL WOMEN

Documents with a female royal title

159 Tell Yamakšedda the wine-carrier, Parnaka spoke as follows:

'2,000 quarts of wine are to be issued to Artystone (Elam. *Irtašduna*) the *dukšiš*. It was ordered by the king.'

Month 1, year 19.

Ansukka wrote the text.

Maraza communicated the message.

PF 1795

160 Tell Harrena the cattle chief, Parnaka spoke as follows:

'Darius the king ordered me, saying: "100 sheep from my estate are to be issued to Artystone the *dukšiš*."' And now Parnaka says: 'As the king ordered me, so I am ordering you. Now you are to issue 100 sheep to Artystone the princess, as was ordered by the king.'

Month 1, year 19.

Ansukka wrote the text

Maraza communicated the message.

Fort.6764

161 Bakeya and Ištin the *dukšiš* received 2 sheep.

PF 823

The first two texts are letters from Persepolis documenting the orders of Darius I to issue wine and sheep to the woman Artystone. Her name is the Greek rendering of the Elamite name Irtašduna, who is known to us as the daughter of Cyrus II and the wife of Darius I (see **177**). Artystone bears the title *dukšiš*, 'princess', which was used as a general term of reference for the female members of the royal family, including the king's wives, sisters and daughters. Both texts are dated to the first month of the 19th year of Darius I, which is March/April 502. Perhaps these vast quantities of foodstuffs were used for the New Year and a special feast celebrated by Darius' wife on this occasion.

The woman Ištin was probably a daughter of Darius I. Bakeya has been identified with Bagaeus, the son of Artontes (Hdt.3.128). This Bagaeus was the father of Mardontes, who served in Xerxes' army in 480/79 (Hdt.7.80).

For Parnaka, the chief economic administrator of Persepolis, who took his orders from the king, see above **140–143**.

Babylonian text documenting a daughter of Xerxes

162 6 *kur* of barley for Artim, the wet-nurse of Ratašah, the daughter of the king, in the care of (the men) Surundu and Ša-pi-kalbi, the chief [...] officials of Artim [...], at the disposal of [...]

Witnesses: [...], [...] son of [...], [... son of] Ahu-iddin; Šumija son of [...]-ahu-iddina.

Scribe: Labaši, son of Nabu-zeru-iddina.

Place: Bit-Sahiran(?)

Accession year of Xerxes, king of Babylon, king of lands.

Evetts 1892: 91 (transl. H. Baker)

This Babylonian document provides a unique reference to an otherwise unknown daughter of Xerxes, Ratašah, whose wet-nurse, Artim, receives a ration of 6 *kur* of grain for an unspecified period of time. The text is dated to 486/5, which means that Ratašah was an infant when Xerxes succeeded to the throne. One *kur* is 151.56 litres. The familial term of reference 'daughter of the king' is also used in the Elamite texts from Persepolis (Elam. *sunki pakri*), see **168**.

Estates of royal women

163 4,260 quarts of flour and grain(?) supplied by Kama-[...] were dispensed on behalf of (the woman) Artystone and of Arsames (Elam. *Iršama*), and was [...]ed.

(In) the *appišdamanna* of (the man) Napumalika.

Year 24. At (the place) Uttiti. (PFS 38)

PF 733

164 Tell Šalamana, the woman Artystone spoke as follows:

'100 quarts of wine are to be issued to the man called Ankama from my estate (Elam. *ulhi*) at Mirandu. Utar is the *hirrakurra*.'

(no date) (PFS 38)

PF 1835

165 Tell Šalamana, Artystone spoke as follows:

'1,000 quarts of wine are to be issued to Kamšabana, the accountant, from Kukkannakan, my estate. Irtima is the *hirrakurra*.'

Year 22, the sealed document (was delivered). (PFS 38)

PF 1836

166 Tell the accountants of (the place) Šullake, Irdabama said this:

'I ordered for Pirmakša, the nurseryman(?), 1,500(?) quarts of grain from my estate. And a parchment document [...] concerning (the place) Raku-[...], he will be making a report. Do you look at the sealed document and do the accounting.'(PFS 51)

PFa 27

In Achaemenid Persia royal women could own estates and had free disposal of the produce. **164** and **165** are letters written on the order of Artystone, to transfer 100 and 1,000 quarts (c.1,000 litres) of wine respectively from two different estates. The letters are sealed with her personal seal (PFS 38). The *hirrakurra* was an official responsible for the delivery of wine. In **163** Artystone is mentioned together with Arsames/Iršama, who is probably to be identified as her son; though the text does not mention an estate, the amount of flour distributed on their order undoubtedly comes from an estate owned by her and her son.

166 is a letter from another woman, named Irdabama. She also orders the withdrawal of food from her own estate. Though she is unknown in Greek sources, the fact that she could own an estate and that she possessed her own personal seal (PFS 51) identifies her as a member of the royal family.

The Persepolis texts verify the information given in Greek sources, that royal women owned land and had the services of cities at their disposal (see **167** and Hdt.2.98.1).

167 'For I myself was once told by a trustworthy person who had been up to their (*the Persians'*) court, that he traversed a very large and fine tract of land, nearly a day's journey, which the inhabitants called the girdle of the king's wife, and another which was similarly called her veil; and many fine and fertile regions reserved for the adornment of the consort; and each of these regions was named after some part of her apparel.'

Plato, *Alcibiades I* 123bc

Socrates, in a dialogue with Alcibiades, refers to land owned by Amestris, the wife of Xerxes (**180**). From a Greek perspective, the fact that Persian noble women could own land was extraordinary, and references are made frequently in Greek texts to this phenomenon. It reflected an exceptional status enjoyed by Persian women—in comparison to Greek women, who could not own land (see also Xen. *An.*1.4.9 for a reference to land owned by Parysatis, the wife of Darius II).

Royal women and travel

168 The wife of Mardonius, a daughter of the king (Elam. *sunki pakri*), received as rations 360 quarts of flour. Daily 90 quarts were received. She received (one at) Kurdusum, (one at) Bessitme, and 2 rations at Liduma. She carried a sealed document of the king. Year 23, month 12.

PFa 5

169 (The woman) Radušdukda, the (wife?) of Gobryas, received as rations for 2 days 360 quarts of flour supplied by Barašiyatiš. She carried a sealed document of the king. Year 23, month 12.

Fort.1017

170 (The woman) Radušnamuya received as rations 176 quarts of wine supplied by Ušaya. For a period of 4 days. She carried a sealed document of the king. Year 23, month 12.

PF 684

171 Gobryas received as rations 300 quarts of beer. Daily 100 quarts were received. He received one (hundred quarts) at Bessitme, two (hundred quarts) at Liduma. He carried a sealed document of the king. Year 23, month 12.

PF 688

172 95 quarts of flour were supplied by Ambaduš.
Zišanduš carried a sealed document of the king and went from Susa to Kandahar. He received 15 quarts, 1 woman 30 quarts, his boys had 10 quarts each. Year 22.

PF 1440

The first four texts issue travel rations for named individuals, who all seem to be part of one travel group, as all the tablets are dated to the same month and year. Further confirmation is found in the mentioning of identical places, Bessitme and Liduma, in **168** and **171**, which are located along the Royal Road between

Persepolis and Susa. Though she is not mentioned by name, the text documents a ration for a daughter of the king, who is the wife of Mardonius (**178**). Her name, Artozostre, is known from Herodotus (**179**). Radušdukda might be the wife of Gobryas (the cuneiform signs are difficult to read here). Perhaps somewhat surprisingly, she daily receives twice as much as Artozostre. If scribal error can be excluded, the ration reflects her extremely high status. Another woman, Radušnamuya, receives a daily ration of 44 quarts of wine, while Gobryas gets 100 quarts of beer per day. Beer and wine are treated as equal liquids, though wine rations occur more commonly. The date of their travel was February/March 499. The texts show that it was possible for women to travel. Neither women nor men travelled on their own, partly for reasons of safety, but also because it was customary to travel in the company of aides and servants. The fifth document, **172**, gives evidence for the travel of a non-royal woman, who travelled in the company of one man and five boys from Susa to Kandahar in Arachosia.

Workers in the service of royal women

173 Workers of the woman Irdabama at Shiraz, whose apportionments are set by (the man) Rašda, received as rations 270 quarts of wine supplied by (the man) Uštana. Months 12, 1, 2, year 19.
1 man 30 (quarts), 2 women 30 (quarts each). Total 3 workers. (PFS 36)

PF 1041

174 90 quarts of wine supplied by Uštana, 1 man and 2 women, total 3 chiefs (Elam. *matištukkašp*), each receives 30 quarts monthly. (PFS 78)

PF 1063

These three workers are employed by Irdabama (see above **166**) at Shiraz, a city 55 km west of Persepolis. The two women and one man receive equal rations of wine throughout the year. Only this special group is defined as *matištukkašp*, 'chiefs'. These workers are mentioned as working only for Irdabama; perhaps they were her personal work force. Seal 78 is the seal of the administrator Uštana.

175 Workers of Irdabama (Elam. *kurtaš Irdabamana*) received as rations at Shiraz 11,100 quarts of grain supplied by (the man) Kuntukka. Their apportionments were set by (the man) Rašda. Month 6, year 22.
62 men (receive) 30 (quarts each), 8 boys 25, 34 boys 20, 26 boys 15 ,19 boys 10, 22 boys 5. 190 women 30, 32 women 20. 11 girls 25, 20 girls 20, 24 girls 15, 17 girls 10, 25 girls 5. Total 480 workers. (PFS 36)

PF 1028

Irdabama employed a large work force at Shiraz. The *kurtaš*, the workers, were identified as her own, being called *kurtaš Irdabamana*, 'workers of Irdabama'. Workers were paid in kind, and the amount of rations depended on their degree of qualification, and, in the case of the children, on their age. In the above text, women and men receive equal amounts of rations. Seal 36 is the official seal of the administrator Rašda.

Marriage alliances

176 They (*the Egyptians*) are well aware (for they know the laws of the Persians better than any other people do), first, that it is their law that no Persian born out of wedlock can become king, and then, that Cambyses was the son of Cassandane, the daughter of Pharnaspes, an Achaemenid, and not of the Egyptian woman.

Herodotus 3.2.2

177 [88.2] Darius married women from the noblest houses of Persia: daughters of Cyrus, Atossa and Artystone. Atossa had been married to her brother Cambyses (*II*) and then to the *magus*; Artystone was a virgin. [88.3] He also married Parmys, the daughter of Cyrus' son Bardiya/Smerdis, as well as the daughter of Otanes (*Phaidyme*), who had found out about the *magus*.

Herodotus 3.88.2–3

178 Mardonius son of Gobryas, who was Xerxes' cousin because he was the child of Darius' sister, and who attended court and had more influence with him than any other Persian, went on giving advice like this.

Herodotus 7.5.1

179 At the beginning of spring (*492*), when the king had deposed his other generals, Mardonius son of Gobryas, who was still a young man and had recently married the daughter of Darius, Artozostre (...).

Herodotus 6.43.1

180 The commander (*of the Persians*) was Otanes, the father of Xerxes' wife Amestris.

Herodotus 7.61.2

The marriage alliances of Darius were politically motivated. By marrying the daughters of his predecessors Cyrus and Bardiya (Atossa, Artystone; Parmys), Darius ensured that they could bear no sons to other Persian nobles, since these sons, as descendants of Cyrus II, would have more claim to the Persian throne than Darius himself. His marriage to Phaidyme, the daughter of Otanes, and his earlier marriage to a daughter of Gobryas (**108**), secured the loyalty of two important Persian families. To tie these bonds even closer, Darius married one of his sisters to Gobryas himself, and another to Otanes (Hdt.7.82). Marriages among the offspring of these alliances included Artozostre's marriage to Mardonius son of Gobryas and Xerxes' marriage to Amestris daughter of Otanes.

　In contrast to the marriages of Darius I and his successors to Persian noble women, the early Persian kings also married daughters of foreign or conquered rulers as part of a political alliance. For example, Cambyses I married Astyages' daughter Mandane (**6**), and Cyrus II is said to have married Amytis, another daughter of Astyages (**10, 40**). Their simultaneous marriages with daughters of noble Persian families ensured the support of the nobility for the king. Such an alliance was concluded in Cyrus' marriage to Cassandane, daughter of Pharnaspes (**176**) and therefore sister of Otanes, according to Herodotus (3.68.1). Early Persian kings practised polygamy out of political necessity. Nothing is known about the ancestors of Artaxerxes' wife Damaspia (**92**), but she was very probably the daughter of a Persian noble couple.

3.4. TRAVEL IN THE EMPIRE
The Royal Roads

181 [52.1] Now the nature of this road is as follows. All along it are the royal stages and excellent inns, and the whole of it passes through country that is inhabited and safe. (...) [53] Thus the total number of stages is a hundred and eleven, and that is the number of resting-places as you go up from Sardis to Susa. If I have rightly reckoned the *parasangs* of the Royal Road, and a *parasang* is thirty furlongs' length (*5-6 km*), which it assuredly is, then between Sardis and the royal palace of Memnon (*Susa*) there are 13,500 furlongs (*1,600 miles*), the number of *parasangs* being four hundred and fifty. And if each day's journey is a hundred and fifty furlongs, then the total of days spent is ninety, neither more nor less.

Herodotus 5.52–53

182 [98.1] Now nothing mortal travels faster than these couriers, by the Persians' skilful contrivance. It is said that the number of men and horses stationed along the road equals the number of days the whole journey takes - a man and a horse for each day's journey; and these are stopped neither by snow nor rain nor heat nor darkness from accomplishing their appointed course with all speed. (...) [98.2] This equestrian post is called in Persian *angareion*.

Herodotus 8.98

183 [6.17] We have observed still another device of Cyrus to cope with the magnitude of his empire; by means of this institution he would speedily discover the condition of affairs, no matter how far distant they might be from him: he experimented to find out how great a distance a horse could cover in a day when ridden hard but not so hard as to break down, and then he erected post-stations at just such distances and equipped them with horses and men to take care of them; at each one of the stations he had the proper official appointed to receive the letters that were delivered and to forward them on, to take in the exhausted horses and riders and send on fresh ones. [6.18] They say, moreover, that sometimes the express does not stop all night, but the night-messengers succeed the day-messengers in relays (...) it is at all events undeniable that this is the fastest overland travelling on earth; and it is a fine thing to have immediate intelligence of everything, in order to attend to it as quickly as possible.

Xenophon, *Cyropaedia* 8.6.17–18

Persian roads were already famous in the fifth century, as Herodotus shows. The system of stations as well as the fast messengers and post-horses ensured an excellent system of communication across the empire. The Persepolis travel texts document extensive travel between Susa and Persepolis, while Herodotus has particular knowledge of the Royal Road between Susa and Sardis. Another route led from Babylon via Ecbatana eastwards to Bactria and India. These roads were designed to carry numerous caravans as well as armies across the empire. Workers were employed to maintain them. They connected the centre of the empire with its subject lands, and allowed an efficient network of communications between the king and his satraps. The Persepolis texts mention ration distributions made to the couriers and post-horses (see below **185-190**).

No satisfactory etymology for the word *angareion* has yet been found. It doubtless comes from an Iranian word, perhaps *(h)ăngăra/u* or *(h)ănkăra/u*, which could mean 'who does/delivers something'.

Travel rations
Rations for individuals
184 From Arsames to Marduk, the officer who is at [...], Nabudalani, the officer, who is at La 'ir, Zatohi, the officer, who is [at] 'Arzuhin, 'Upastabar, the officer who is at Arbel, Halsu(?) and Mat-al-Ubaš(?), Bagafarna, the officer who is at Sa'lam, Fradafarna and Gavazana(?), the officers who are at Damascus:

'And now, behold! One named Nehtihur, (my) officer, is going to Egypt. Give (him as) provisions from my estate in your province every day two measures of white meal, three measures of inferior(?) meal, two measures of wine or beer, and one sheep, and for his servants, 10 men, one measure of meal daily for each, (and) hay according to (the number of) his horses; and give provisions for two Cilicians (and) one craftsman, all three my servants, who are going with him to Egypt, for each and every man daily one measure of meal; give them these provisions, each officer among you in turn, in accordance with (the stages of) his journey from province to province until he reaches Egypt; and if he is more than one day in any (one) place, do not thereafter assign them more provisions for those days.'

Bagasrava is cognizant of this order: Rašt is the clerk.

Driver 1967: no.6

The correspondence of the Persian Arsames (see on **84**) was written in Aramaic. The surviving letters were written between 428 and 406. While some were written on papyrus, a group of letters, found in a leather pouch, was written on leather scrolls. These letters were written during Arsames' absence from Egypt, and are concerned with the administration of Arsames' estates there. These estates, largely situated in the western Delta, were administered by a steward, who is named in this letter as Nehtihur. Letter 6 documents an order of the satrap of Egypt, Arsames, to provide his steward with daily food rations from his estates consisting of an amount of flour, wine or beer and one sheep. The letter also takes care of the provisions for servants, the horses, and craftsmen. Such a document was the authorisation for an official to travel across the empire. It was the first in a chain of administrative documents which registered the supply of food rations for each traveller at each royal storehouse he passed on his way to his destination and back. These documents finally ended up with the administration in Persepolis, where the storehouses had to account for their expenditure of wine and flour (see below **185-190**).

Fast messengers and élite guides

185 Muška received 1" quarts of flour, supplied by Bakadušda, as a fast messenger (Elam. *pirradaziš*). He went from the king to Ziššawiš. He carried a sealed document from the king. Month 10.

PF 1285

186 Išbaramištima received 100 quarts of flour and gave (them) as rations to Abbatema the Indian. (Išbaramištima is) the one who crosses the land as an élite guide (Elam. *barrišdama lakkukra*). Month 1, year 23.

PF 1317

187 Abbatema received 110 quarts of flour. As his daily ration he receives 70 quarts. 20 men each receive 2 quarts. He carried a sealed document from the king. They went forth from India. They went to Susa. Month 2, year 23.
Išbaramištima is his élite guide. The seal of Išbaramištima was applied (to this tablet).

PF 1318

188 Turpiš the caravan leader (Elam. *karabattiš*) received 3" quarts of flour supplied by Karma and gave (them) to 1 gentleman and 2 servants. Month 9, year 22.

PF 1341

189 Dauma received 465 quarts of flour. 23 men each (received) 1" quarts. 12 boys each received 1 quart. He carried a sealed document of Artaphernes (Elam. *Irdapirna*). They went forth from Sardis (Elam. *Išparda*) to Persepolis. Month 9, year 27. (At) Hidali.

PF 1404

190 400 quarts of grain were received and delivered as fodder for one(?) express horse. Year 20.

PF 1700

Travel rations were issued to individuals and groups of people travelling on official business across the empire. An official document allowed them to receive a daily amount of food from the royal supply stations for the duration of their journey. Travellers are attested coming from Persis and southern Elam, some from the East (**172, 186**). Other texts mention journeys from Bactria, Aria, Kerman, Egypt, Sardis, Babylon, and Arabia.

The travel texts reflect a highly developed system of travel, transport and communication. Travellers were accompanied by guides **186, 187**). The texts also attest caravan leaders (**188**) and fast messengers (**185**). Travellers were accompanied by camels, mules, and horses, which also received daily rations of fodder and even wine. Their food supply also was rationed for the duration of the journey and recorded by the scribes of the royal storehouses.

The procedure for documenting travel rations was as follows. Travel texts were inscribed at the supply station and sent to Persepolis. There the commodities dispensed were credited to the account of the supplier and debited to the account of the official who had provided the travellers with a sealed document (Elam. *halmi*) or an authorisation (Elam. *miyatukkam*). The authorisation official was sometimes located far from

Persepolis, as in the case of Artaphernes, the brother of Darius, who was the satrap of Sardis between 511 and 492 (**189**; PF 1455). For Hidali, see **56**.

3.5. RELIGION IN THE EMPIRE
The *daiva*-inscription

191 §1. Ahura Mazda is a great god, who created this earth, who created the sky, who created man, who created happiness for man, who made Xerxes king, one king of many, one lord of many.

§2. I am Xerxes, the Great King, king of kings, king of countries containing many men, king of this great earth far and wide, son of Darius the king, an Achaemenid, a Persian, son of a Persian, an Aryan, son of Aryan lineage.

§3. Xerxes the king says: 'By the favour of Ahura Mazda these are the countries of which I am king outside Persia. I ruled over them, they brought me tribute, they did what I told them. My law (OP *dāta*) held them firm: Media, Elam, Arachosia, Armenia, Drangiana, Parthia, Aria, Bactria, Sogdiana, Chorasmia, Babylonia, Assyria, Sattagydia, Sardis, Egypt, Ionians—those who dwell by the sea, and those who dwell across the sea—men of Maka, Arabia, Gandara, Sind, Cappadocia, Dahae, Amyrgian Scythians, pointed-cap Scythians, Skudra, men of Akaufaka, Libyans, Carians, Ethiopians.'

§4. Xerxes the king says: 'When I became king, there was one among these countries which are inscribed above, (one which) was in commotion. Afterwards Ahura Mazda brought me aid. By the favour of Ahura Mazda I struck that country and subdued it.

§5. 'Among these countries there was a place where previously demons (OP *daivas*) had been worshipped. Afterwards, by the favour of Ahura Mazda, I destroyed that sanctuary of demons, and I made a proclamation: "The demons had been worshipped." Where previously the demons had been worshipped, there I worshipped Ahura Mazda in accordance with Truth reverently.

§6. 'And there were other matters which had been done badly. These I made good. All that I did, I did by the favour of Ahura Mazda. Ahura Mazda brought me aid until I had completed the work.

§7. 'You who will be there after me, if you think: "Happy may I be when living, and when dead may I be blessed", have respect for the law which Ahura Mazda has established, and worship Ahura Mazda in accordance with Truth reverently. The man who has respect for the law which Ahura Mazda has established and worships Ahura Mazda in accordance with Truth reverently becomes both happy while living and blessed when dead.'

§8. Xerxes the king says: 'May Ahura Mazda protect me from harm, and my royal house, and this land. This I pray of Ahura Mazda, this may Ahura Mazda give me.'

XPh

The trilingual inscription, written on stone tablets, was found in a building in the southeast of the royal terrace of Persepolis. Two copies exist written in Old Persian, one copy was written in Elamite and one in Babylonian. Another copy written in Old Persian was found in Pasargadae, where it had been re-used to cover a drain. Following the formula of royal inscriptions known from Darius I, Xerxes invokes the support of Ahura Mazda. In a wording which sounds somewhat firmer and more determined than the phrases used by Darius, Xerxes proudly demonstrates his power over the lands of the empire (§3).

Paragraphs 4 and 5 turn to the central issue of the inscription. First, Xerxes had to put down a rebellion in one of the lands. Following that statement, Xerxes refers, or seems to refer, to a specific country which did not worship Ahura Mazda, but false gods or demons. As a reaction, Xerxes destroyed their sanctuaries and replaced their cults with that of Ahura Mazda. This remark has been interpreted to mean that Xerxes showed religious intolerance, imposing the cult of Ahura Mazda forcibly on people. It also implies that no other cult was tolerated. The image that Xerxes is given in Herodotus supports that interpretation. Xerxes' *hybris* and disrespect for alien gods was evident in his destruction of Greek temples and in his removal of the statue of Bel-Marduk in Babylon (**200**). But the allegations made in the Greek sources can be refuted: in his peace negotiations with Athens in 479 Mardonius offered to rebuild the temples (Hdt.8.140.2), and Xerxes did not remove a divine statue from the temple in Babylon. Greek propaganda against Xerxes may be understandable, but it does not reflect historical truth.

To return to Xerxes' inscription, he does not identify the land which supposedly worshipped false gods. While Babylon might seem the obvious land for his measures (the revolt of Belšimanni in 482/1 (**66**) and perhaps that of Šamaš-eriba in 479), Bactria is an equally likely candidate (see Hdt 9.113.2), as is Egypt.

A different understanding of the inscription is achieved by aligning it with other royal inscriptions. All royal inscriptions try to convey eternal truths about the Persian king, his kingship and his empire. The purpose of the inscriptions is not to record individual political events, but to emphasise the king's divine rule and the peace of the empire, secured by following the Truth and adhering to the moral values of Ahura Mazda. In this light, it is possible that instead of referring to a particular event, Xerxes affirmed the major law which secured the peace of the empire: loyalty to the king. Disloyalty leads to revolt and means the upheaval of the empire. It will be punished severely: the 'religious tolerance', which is assured as long as peace prevails, will cease, and the sanctuaries of those who rebel will be destroyed. The message becomes clear: loyalty to the king is met with tolerance for local cults and religious ceremonies, disloyalty means that these liberties will be curtailed. These are the *dāta*, the laws made by Ahura Mazda (§7); they ensure that man enjoys happiness and peace, even in his afterlife.

Šatin and *magus*

192   Turkama the priest (Elam. *šatin*) received 57 quarts of wine supplied by Ušaya and used them for the gods: 7 quarts for Ahura Mazda, 20 quarts for the (*Elamite*) god Humban, 10 quarts for the river Huputiš, 10 quarts for the river Rannakarra, 10 quarts for the river Šaušaunuš.

                                                                                        PF 339

193   Hatarbanuš the *magus* (Elam. *makuš*) received 300 quarts of wine supplied by Ašbaštiya for the libation of the *lan* (*religious ceremony*) for one year. Year 23. At Ankarakkan.

                                                                                        PF 759

194   Yašda the *haturmakša* (official at) Matezziš received 40 quarts of flour supplied by Upirradda (for) the *tamšiyam* of the *lan* ceremony. Year 23, month 7.

                                                                                        PF 762

The Persepolis Fortification texts document that Assyrian, Elamite and Iranian gods were worshipped in Persis. They also testify to the fact that mountains and rivers were regarded as sacred and that sacrifices were made to them (see Mt. Bisitun as the 'place of the gods', above **44**). Different officials were involved in the religious ceremonies, most prominently the *šatin*, the *magus*, and the *haturmakša*. As **192** exemplifies, the *šatin* was responsible for sacrificing to the foreign gods worshipped in Persia, as well as to the god Ahura Mazda and to mountains and rivers. The word *šatin* is probably best translated as 'priest'.

The responsibilities of a *magus* were different from those of a *šatin*. In PF 759 the *magus* performs the *lan* ceremony. This has been understood to be a religious ceremony linked with Ahura Mazda, yet none of the texts referring to the *lan* ceremony specifies the deity or deities for whom this ritual was performed. Besides performing the *lan* ceremony, a *magus* also sacrificed to rivers and mountains (PF 1955: 1.1). Since Ahura Mazda, who appears in only a few texts from Persepolis, receives sacrifice from *šatins*, the notion that the *magi* were connected with the cult of Ahura Mazda, has to be dismissed. Instead it appears that the *magi* upheld the religious ceremonies of the Median population of Persia, ensuring the continuity of Median cults and the worship of Median gods.

Sometimes a *magus* bears an additional title, which can be either *haturmakša*, or *pirramašda*. The word *haturmakša* may derive from an Old Persian word **atrvaxša*, 'fire-fanner', while *pirramašda* has been explained as deriving from Old Persian **framazda-*, 'one who memorises'. These terms may refer to special tasks (or offices) carried out by individuals who were also *magi*.

Evidence from Egypt
Hieroglyphic inscriptions from el-Khargeh

195 The Good God, Lord of the Two Lands, lord of the cult, King of Upper and Lower Egypt, Son of Re, Lord of the Crowns (*of Egypt*), given eternal life like the Sun forever, beloved of Amun, the Lord of Hibis, Great God, mighty of strength, beloved of Mut, the Lady of Hibis, and beloved of Khonsu [...] in Hibis.
He has made this monument for his father Amun-Re, Lord of Hibis, Great God, mighty of strength, together with his Ennead of the gods, building for him this temple anew, in fine limestone of Meska, and erecting the gates made of pine wood from the western mountains, the name of which is *pr-šn*; and covering [their fittings with bronze] from Asia; renovating his temple as it had been originally. May they give him hundreds of thousands of anniversaries, and celebrate the jubilees on the throne of Horus, at the head of the living, like the Sun for ever and ever!

Droiton 1940: 340

196 The disc of Amun-Re goes forth in life and power at dawn, illuminating the Two Lands (*of Egypt*) through the perfection of his eyes. (...) The god rejoices when he sees the august, beautiful, and efficacious mansion of his temple complex. There is no other sovereign who is as great as the king of Upper and Lower Egypt, Son of Re, Darius, Great King of all rulers' lands. He has made as his monument to his (divine) father Amenebis (*Re*), Great God, strong-of-arm, making for him (...) of fine limestone of Meska, the eternal place. It was (the goddess) Seshat who founded its walls, which were constructed with excellent skill for all time. It was the One south of this wall (*the god Ptah*) who crafted its art work and created the perfection of its doorways, through which the sun shines for ever and ever.

Droiton 1940: 360

Darius rebuilt a temple of Amun-Re at el-Khargeh (Hibis), northwest of the First Cataract of the Nile. The first text is inscribed on the outer wall of the temple, praising the building work of Darius for the Egyptian god. The second text addresses Darius as the pharaoh of Egypt, honouring him with several epithets.

Funerary inscription on a stele from Saqqara
197

Spell Osiris, the foremost of the West, the Great God, lord of the temple, (may) he give an invocation-offering of bread, beer, oxen, fowl, clothing, alabaster(?), incense(?), things perfect and pure, the luxuries upon which the god lives, to the *ka* of Djerbherbes, son of Artam, born of the lady Tanofrether.

Mathiesen et al. 1995:35

The funerary stele was found at the north wall of the Gisr el-Mudir (Great Enclosure) in Saqqara, an area with tombs from the Old Kingdom period. The stele is dated to the time of the Persian occupation of Egypt, and in all likelihood dates to the first occupation, between 525 and 404. The stele bears a hieroglyphic inscription and a demotic text, which is less well preserved but with a wording similar to that of the hieroglyphic text. Djerbherbes, in whose honour this gravestone was erected, is the son of a Persian, called Artam, and an Egyptian lady called Tanofrether. The name Djerbherbes is Egyptian. Since it is highly uncommon for

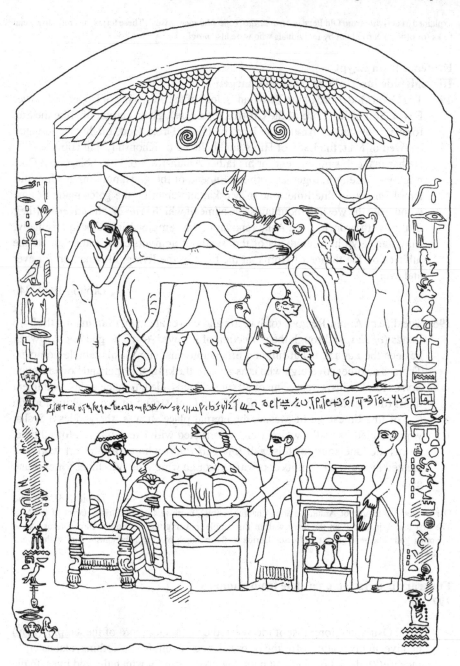

12. Stele from Saqqara

an Egyptian to take on a Persian name, the stele documents a rare glimpse into a union between a high Persian official, Artam, and a foreigner. In Egyptian religion *ka* is the vitality of a man, which leaves the body at the point of death and is reunited with it in the next world. The scene depicts a high-ranking Persian seated on a throne, being approached by two figures whose dress is Egyptian. The Persian is depicted wearing Persian clothes and seated on a Persian throne, his feet resting on a footstool. The lower scene is reminiscent of the Persepolis reliefs in which the seated king is depicted in an audience scene, though it is not sufficiently consistent to allow the identification of the seated figure with the Persian king himself. It could be the Persian satrap, who is approached by the offerer of the stele, Djerbherbes, but it is also possible that Artam himself, the father of Djerbherbes, is approached in this scene by his own son.

Greek evidence on Persian Religion
Darius' letter to Gadatas
198 The King of Kings, Darius, son of Hystaspes, speaks to Gadatas, his slave, thus:
'I find that you are not completely obedient concerning my orders. Because you are cultivating my land, transplanting fruit trees from the province Beyond-the-Euphrates to the western Asiatic regions, I praise your purpose, and in consequence there will be laid up in store for you great favour in the royal house. But because my religious dispositions are nullified by you, I shall give you, unless you make a change, proof of a wronged (king's) anger. For the gardeners sacred to Apollo have been made to pay tribute to you; and land which is profane they have dug up at your command. You are ignorant of my ancestors' attitude to the god, who told the Persians all of the truth and [...]'

ML no.12; Fornara 35

The text is probably based on an original Persian text. It is addressed to Gadatas, who most likely was the satrap of the province of Ionia. The Greek text refers to him as slave (*doulos*), but it would be more appropriate to call him a subject of the king. He is praised by Darius for his efforts to cultivate land in Ionia with fruit trees imported from the province 'Beyond-the-Euphrates'. Near Eastern and biblical texts know the province as 'Across-the River' (Syria-Palestine). The rewards Darius offers Gadatas in return for his work may include the honour of becoming a King's Friend or receiving royal gifts (see above **116–122**), either of which would declare his new status at court.

Darius is displeased with Gadatas for collecting tribute from the sacred gardens of Apollo and ordering their gardeners to work on profane soil. With the official respect paid to non-Persian gods, Darius follows the religious policy of his predecessors. The acceptance and recognition of foreign gods meant the continuation of the religious and cultural traditions of the different peoples in the satrapies.

Herodotus' view
199 [131.1] The customs which I know the Persians observe are these: They do not set up statues of gods, temples or altars; those who do so they regard as behaving foolishly, because, I suppose, they do not believe that the gods have the same nature as men, as the Greeks think. [131.2] They call the whole firmament Zeus, and to him they offer sacrifice on the mountain tops. They also sacrifice to the sun and moon, earth and fire, water and winds. [131.3] These are the only gods that they have sacrificed to from ancient times; later they learned from the Assyrians and Arabians to sacrifice to the Heavenly Goddess (*Aphrodite*). She is called by the Assyrians Mylitta, by the Arabians Alilat, by the Persians Mitra.
[132.1] To these gods the Persians offer sacrifice as follows: they neither build altars nor kindle fire, nor do they pour libations; there is no piping, no putting on of chaplets, no sprinkling of barley; but a man leads his victim to a purified space and then calls on the god he wishes to sacrifice to, himself wearing round his cap a wreath, usually of myrtle. [132.2] The sacrificer is not allowed to pray for blessings for himself alone, rather he prays for the well-being of the king and all the Persians, among whom he himself is included. He then cuts the victim into portions and having boiled the flesh places it on the softest greenery that he can find, clover by choice. [132.3] When he has so displayed it, a *magus* comes and chants over it the hymn about the birth of the gods, which is how the Persians describe it. No sacrifice can be offered without a *magus*. After a little while the sacrificer carries away the flesh of the victim and does what he likes with it.

Herodotus 1.131–132

Herodotus' information about Persian religious practices is only partly correct. Sacrifices will have taken place on mountains, probably for the mountain itself (192). The Persians also worshipped the natural elements, earth, water, wind and fire, as well as the sun and the moon. It is also the case that no temples were built for the gods in Achaemenid Persia, but altars were erected to place offerings on or to burn a fire for the god. One such altar is depicted in the reliefs on the royal tombs of the Achaemenid kings at Naqš-e Rustam. There the king is depicted standing on a platform, his hands raised in a gesture of worship, before a fire altar, which itself stands on a stepped platform. It is also known from the Persepolis Fortification texts that the Persians poured libations for the gods. Animal sacrifice likewise is attested to have been offered by Persian priests. In light of the evidence from the Persepolis Fortification texts it must be doubted, however, whether the Persian priests who had to be present were exclusively *magi*, since these were concerned with only certain cults, while the *šatins* were priests who performed sacrifices for many gods, including Ahura Mazda. Herodotus does not know the name of the principal god of the Persian kings, but refers to him as 'Zeus'. He also mistakes the Iranian god Mithra for a goddess. The cult of Mithra, the sun god and god of treaties, may have already been practised in certain regions of the Persian empire, but his cult was elevated to a royal cult only by the time of Artaxerxes II.

Xerxes and the Babylonian temples

200 [183.2] Outside the temple (*of Bel in Babylon*) is a golden altar, as well as another great altar, on which fully grown victims are sacrificed. On the golden altar only sucklings may be sacrificed, but on the larger altar the Chaldaeans yearly offer frankincense weighing a thousand talents when they celebrate the feast of this god. In the time of Cyrus, there was still in the precinct a statue of a man (Gr. *andrias*), twelve cubits high (*6m*) and made of solid gold. [183.3] I did not see it myself, but I repeat what the Chaldaeans told me. Darius son of Hystaspes intended to remove this statue, but did not dare; but Xerxes son of Darius did take it and killed the priest who tried to prevent him.

Herodotus 1.183.2–3

This passage has often been interpreted as meaning that Xerxes committed a sacrilege in the temple of Babylon by removing the statue of the city god Bel-Marduk. This claim supported the idea of the *hybris* of Xerxes, who showed disrespect for the gods and religious cults. But Herodotus speaks of the statue of a human figure (Gr. *andrias*), not of a divinity (Gr. *agalma*). Later Greek sources speak of Xerxes' destruction of the temples of Babylon (see Arr. *An*.3.16.4; Strabo 16.1.5) only to contrast Xerxes' wilfulness with the nobility of Alexander.

The Jews under Persian rule
Return of the exiles from Babylon

201 He (*Nebuchadnezzar*) carried into exile in Babylon the remnant who had escaped from the sword, and they became slaves to him and his sons until the kingdom of Persia came to power.

2 Chronicles 36.20

Nebuchadnezzar (Bab. *Nabu-kudurri-usur*) was king of Babylon from 604 to 562. His reign was marked by continuous campaigns that he led over ten years, fighting in Syria and Palestine, and unsuccessfully attacking Egypt in 601. In December 598 he led a campaign against Judah, and on 16 March 597 he took Jerusalem. The Jewish king Jehoiachin and many of his subjects were deported as prisoners to Babylon. This was followed by more deportations in 587/6 and 582/1. The deportation of the Jews under Nebuchadnezzar is recorded in *Kings*, *Chronicles* and *Ezra*.

202 In the first year of Cyrus, king of Persia, in order to fulfil the word of the Lord spoken by Jeremiah, the Lord moved the heart of Cyrus, king of Persia, to make a proclamation throughout his realm and to put it in writing: 'This is what Cyrus, king of Persia, says: "The Lord, the God of heaven, has given me all the kingdoms of the earth, and he has appointed me to build him a temple in Jerusalem in Judah. To anyone of his people among you - I say God be with him, and let him go up to Jerusalem in Judah and rebuild the temple of the Lord (...)'" Then the family heads of Judah and Benjamin, and the priests and the Levites (...) prepared to go and rebuild the house of the Lord in Jerusalem.

Ezra 1.1–5

After the Persian conquest of Babylon in 539, Cyrus II allowed the return of the exiled Jews in Babylon. Cyrus is traditionally credited with issuing permission for the Jews to rebuild the temple in Jerusalem. This project came to a halt during the reign of Artaxerxes I, but was continued under his successor Darius II, and paid for by the royal treasury, when a copy of Cyrus' decree concerning the rebuilding of the temple was found in the archives of Ecbatana. (*Ezra* 6.1–5). We have to dismiss the assumption made in this passage that Cyrus issued his proclamation out of respect for Yahweh: his policy towards the Jewish deportees in Babylon ought to be seen in the same light as his restoration of the cult of Marduk in Babylon, namely, as a political means to win the support of the subject peoples.

203 This is a copy of the letter king Artaxerxes had given to Ezra the priest and scribe, a man learned in matters concerning the commands and decrees that the Lord laid upon Israel:
Artaxerxes, king of kings, to Ezra the priest and teacher of the law of the God of heaven:
'I now decree that any of the Israelites in my kingdom, including priests and Levites, who wish to go to Jerusalem with you, may go. You are sent by the king and his seven advisers to enquire about Judah and Jerusalem with regard to the law of your God, with which you are entrusted. Moreover, you take with you the silver and gold that the king and his advisers have freely given to the God of Israel, whose dwelling is in Jerusalem, together with all the silver and gold you may obtain from the province of Babylon, as well as the freewill offering of the people and the priests for the temple of their God in Jerusalem. With this money be sure to buy bulls, rams, and male lambs, together with grain offerings and drink offerings, and sacrifice them on the altar of the temple of your God in Jerusalem.'

Ezra 7.11–17

Ezra, who was an official for Jewish affairs at the royal court, was appointed by Artaxerxes to go to Jerusalem and look into the religious affairs of the Jewish community.

204 In the month Nisannu, in the twentieth year of king Artaxerxes, when wine was brought for him, I (*Nehemiah*) took the wine and gave it to him. (...) The king said to me: 'What is it you want?' Then I prayed to the God of heaven and I answered the king: 'If it pleases Your Majesty the king (...) send me to the city in Judah where my fathers are buried so that I can rebuild it.' Then the king, with his queen sitting beside him, asked me: 'How long will your journey take and when will you return?' It pleased the king to send me; so I set a time.

Nehemiah 2.1-6

Nehemiah was the king's cupbearer. In March 445 he was allowed to return to Jerusalem to oversee the rebuilding of the walls of the city. He returned to Susa after twelve years.

Elephantine

205 To our Lord Bagohi, governor of Judah, from your servants Yedonyah and his colleagues, the priests of Elephantine- the-fortress. May the God of heaven seek after the health of our Lord forever! May he give you favour before Darius (*II*) the king and the members of the royal house! May he grant you long life! May you be happy and prosper forever! Now, your servant Yedonyah and his colleagues speak thus:

In the month Tammuz, year 14 of Darius (*II*) (*14 July - 13 August 410*), when Arsames had left and gone to the king, the priests of Hnub, the god who resides at Elephantine-the-fortress, gave silver and goods to Vidranga, the governor who was here, saying: 'Let them remove the temple of Yahu the God, which is in Elephantine-the-fortress, from there!' Then the villain Vidranga sent a letter to Nafaina, his son, who was commander of the garrison of Syene-the-fortress, saying: "Let them destroy the temple of Yahu, which is in Elephantine-the-fortress!" Then Nafaina led the Egyptians together with other forces; they came into the fortress of Elephantine with their weapons, they entered the temple, they rased it to the ground, and they broke the stone pillars which were there. It also occurred that they destroyed the five doorways of stone, built with hewn blocks of stone, which were in that temple, and they lifted off their doors and the hinges of those doors, which were in bronze, and the roof of cedar wood, all of it, together with the rest of the furniture and other things that were there, all of it they burnt with fire. And the pieces of gold and silver, and everything that was in the temple, all of it, they took and made their own. It was in the days of the kings of Egypt that our fathers had built this temple at Elephantine, and when Cambyses (*II*) entered Egypt, he found this temple built, and they overthrew all the temples of the gods of Egypt, but nobody damaged anything in this temple. When this was done, we with our wives and our children put on sackcloth and fasted and prayed to Yahu the Lord of heaven, who let us see our desire inflicted upon that villain Vidranga. (...)

Look upon your well-wishers and friends who are here in Egypt and send a letter from you to them concerning the temple of the God Yahu to build it in Elephantine-the-fortress, as it was built before, and they shall offer the meal-offering and incense and sacrifice on the altar of the God Yahu on your behalf, and we will pray for you at all times, we, our wives, our children, and all the Jews who are here. (...) Also Arsames knew nothing of all this which was done to us. On day 20 of the month Marheshwan, year 17 (*26 November 407*) of Darius (*II*) the king.

Driver 1967, no.30

This letter was sent by the Jewish community of Elephantine to the governor of Judah at the time of the reign of Darius II. Yedonyah and his colleagues refer to the destruction of the temple in Elephantine by Vidranga and his son Nafaina in 410, when Arsames, the satrap of Egypt (see on **84, 184**), was outside the province. Yedonyah is concerned that no permission has been given to restore the temple, even though three years have elapsed since its destruction. Note the reference to Cambyses' conquest of Egypt. The temple, so Yedonyah states, was built before Cambyses came to Egypt in 525, and, more importantly, Cambyses seems to have respected the temple. Though the reference is slight, it does shed a very different light on the religious policy of Cambyses from the distorted view given in Herodotus (see **25, 26**).

BIBLIOGRAPHY

Balcer, J.M., (1987), *Herodotus and Bisitun, Stuttgart* (Historia Einzelschriften, 49).

Berger, P.R., (1975), 'Der Kyros-Zylinder mit dem Zusatzfragment BIN II Nr 32 und die akkadischen Namen im Danielbuch', *.0* 64:192–234.

Bowman, R.A., (1970), *Aramaic Ritual Texts from Persepolis*, Chicago.

Bresciani, E., (1998), 'L'Egitto achemenide Dario I e il canale del mar Rosso', *Transeuphratène* 14: 103–111.

Briant, P., (1992), 'La date des révoltes babylonniennes contre Xerxès', *StIr* 21: 7–20.

Briant, P. (1996), *De Cyrus à Alexandre*, Paris.

Brosius, M., (1998), *Women in Ancient Persia (559-331 BC)*, Oxford.

Cardascia, G., (1951), *Les Archives de Murašû: Une famille d'hommes d'affaires babyloniens à l'époque perse (455-403 av. J.-C.)*, Paris.

Cowley, A.E., (1923), *Aramaic Papyri of the Fifth Century BC*, Oxford.

Devauchelle, D., (1994), 'Les stèles du Sérapéum de Memphis conservées au musée du Louvre', in: *Acta Demotica. Acts of the Fifth International Conference for Demotists*, Pisa, 95–114.

Devauchelle, D., (1995), 'Le sentiment chez les anciens Égyptiens', *Transeuphratène* 9: 67–80.

Drews, R., (1974), 'Sargon, Cyrus, and Mesopotamian Folk History', *JNES* 33: 387–93.

Droiton, E., (1940), 'Inscriptions de Darius Ier au temple de Khargeh', *ASAE* 40: 339–377.

Driver, G.R. (1965), *Aramaic Documents of the Fifth Century BC*, Oxford.

Eilers, W., (1974), 'Le texte cunéiforme du cylindre de Cyrus', *AcIr* 2: 25–31.

Evetts, B.T.A., (1892), *Babylonische Texte, Heft VIB: Inscriptions of the reigns of Evil-Merodach (BC 562–559), Neriglissar (BC 559–555) and Laborosoarchod (BC 555)*, Leipzig.

Garrison, M., (1991), 'Seals and the elite at Persepolis. Some observations on early Achaemenid Persian Art,' *Ars Orientalis* 21: 1–29.

Garrison, M., (1998), 'The Seals of Ašbazana (Aspathines)', *AchHist* 11:115–131.

Graf, D.F., (1994), 'The Persian Royal Road System', *AchHist* 8:167–189.

Grayson, A.K., (1975), *Assyrian and Babylonian Chronicles*, Locust Valley, N.Y.

Greenfield, J.C., B.Porten, (1982), *The Aramaic Version of the Inscription of Bisitun*, London.

Grillot-Susini, F., (1990), 'Les textes de fondation du palais se Suse', *JA* 218: 213–222

Hallock, R.T., (1969), *Persepolis Fortification Tablets*, Chicago.

Hallock, R.T. (1978), 'Selected Fortification Texts', *Cah.D.A.F.I.* 8: 109–36.

Hinz, W., (1950), 'The Elamite Version of the Record of Darius's Palace at Susa', *JNES* 9: 1–7.

Hodjache, S., O. Berlev, (1977), 'Le sceau de Cambyse', *Chronique d'Egypte* 52/103: 37–9.

Kent R.G., (1953), *Old Persian. Grammar, Texts, Lexicon*, New Haven.

King, L. W., R.C. Thompson, (1907), *The Sculptures and Inscription of Darius the Great on the Rock of Behistûn in Persia*, London.

Kuhrt, A., (1983), 'The Cyrus Cylinder and Achaemenid Imperial Policy', *JSOT* 25: 83–97.

Kuhrt, A., (1995), *The Ancient Near East*, 2 vols., London.

Lecoq, P., (1997), *Les inscriptions de la Perse achéménide*, Paris.

Lewis, D.M., (1977), *Sparta and Persia*, Leiden.

Lewis, D.M., (1980), 'Datis the Mede', *JHS* 100:194-5.

Lewis D.M., (1985), 'Persians in Herodotus', in *The Greek Historians. Literature and History, Papers presented to A.E. Raubitschek*, Palo Alto, CA.: 101–107.

Lichtheim, M., (1960), *Ancient Egyptian Literature. A Book of Readings. Vol.3: The Late Period*, Berkeley, Los Angeles, London.

Mathiesen, I., E. Bettles, S. Davies, H.S. Smith, (1995), 'A stela of the Persian period from Saqqara', *Journal of Egyptian Archaeology* 81: 23–41.

Mayrhofer, M., (1978), *Supplement zur Sammlung der altpersischen Inschriften*, Wien, 28–29.

Mayrhofer, M., (1995), *Etymologisches Wörterbuch des Altindoarischen II*, Lieferung 18, Heidelberg.

Scheil, V., (1929), *Inscriptions des Achéménides à Suse*, Paris (MDP 21).

Parker, R.A., W.H. Dubberstein, (1938), *Babylonian Chronology 626 BC–AD 45*, Chicago.

Posener, G., (1936), *La première domination perse en Égypte*, Cairo.

Potts, D.T., (1999), *The Archaeology of Elam: Formation and Transformation of an Ancient Iranian State*, Cambridge.

Sancisi-Weerdenburg, H., (1998), 'Bāji', *AchHist* 11: 23–34.

Schmitt, R., (1967), 'Medisches und persisches Sprachgut bei Herodot', *ZDMG* 117: 119–145.

Schmitt, R., (1971), "Méconnaisance' altiranischen Sprachgutes im Griechischen', *Glotta* 49: 95–110.

Schmitt, R., (1976), 'Der Titel 'Satrap'', in: *Studies in Greek, Italic, and Indo-European Linguistics offered to L.R. Palmer on the Occasion of his 70th Birthday June 5, 1976*, ed by A. Morpurgo Davies and W. Meid, Innsbruck.

Schmitt, R., (1978), *Die Iranier-Namen bei Aischylos*, Wien. (Iranica Graeca Vetustiora. Veröffentlichungen der Iranischen Kommission , 6).

Schmitt, R., (1981), Altpersische Siegelinschriften, Wien.

Schmitt, R., (1982), 'Achaemenid Throne-names', *AION* 42/1: 83–95.

Schmitt, R., (1991), *The Bisitun Inscriptions of Darius the Great*. Old Persian Text, London.

Spiegelberg, W., (1914), *Die sogenannte demotische Chronik*, Leipzig.

Starr, C., (1975, 1977), 'Greeks and Persians in the Fourth Century BC: A Study in Cultural Contacts before Alexander', *IrAnt* 11: 39–99; 12: 49-115.

Stolper, M.W., (1983), 'The Death of Artaxerxes I', *AMI* 16: 223–236.

Stolper, M.W., (1989), 'The Governor of Babylon and Across-the-River in 486 BC', *JNES* 48: 284–305.

Strassmeier, J.N., (1889), 'Inschriften von Nabopalassar und Smerdis', *ZA* 4: 123–8.

Strassmeier, J.N., (1890), *Inschriften von Cambyses, König von Babylon*, Leipzig.

Stronach, D., (1989), 'The Royal Garden at Pasargadae: Evolution and Legacy', in: Meyer, L., E. de Haerinck (eds.), *Archeologica iranica et orientalis. Miscellanea in honorem Louis Vanden Berghe*, 2 vols., Ghent: 475–502,

Vallat, F., (1970), 'Table élamite de Darius I', *RA* 64: 149–160.

Vallat, F., (1971), 'Deux nouvelles 'Chartes de fondation' d'un palais de Darius 1er à Suse', *Syria* 48: 53–9.

Vallat, F., (1977), *Corpus des inscriptions royales en élamite achéménide*, PhD.Paris (unpubl.).

Vallat, F., (1974), 'L'inscription trilingue de Xerxes à la porte de Darius', *Cah.D.A.F.I.* 4: 171–180.

Voigtlander, E. von (1978), *The Bisitun Inscription of Darius the Great. Babylonian Version*, London.

Wiesehöfer, J., (1980), 'Die 'Freunde' und 'Wohltäter' des Grosskönigs', *StIr* 11: 17–21.

Wiesehöfer, J., (1996), *Ancient Persia*, London.

Yamauchi, E.M., (1990), *Persia and the Bible*, Grand Rapids.

Yardley, J.C., (1994), *Justin. Epitome of the Philippic History of Pompeius Trogus*, Atlanta, GA.

Printed in the United States
by Baker & Taylor Publisher Services